I Killed A Bluebird

Other Books By This Author

The Kitchen Traveler Cookbook

Writing as Jim L. Traveler

The St. Croix Incident

I Killed A Bluebird

James L. Winfree

Authors Choice Press
New York Lincoln Shanghai

I Killed A Bluebird

Authors Choice Press
an imprint of iUniverse, Inc.

For information address:
iUniverse
2021 Pine Lake Road, Suite 100
Lincoln, NE 68512
www.iuniverse.com

ISBN: 0-595-27067-0

Printed in the United States of America

TO

My Grandsons

Robert Barry Winfree

Braden Lancaster Winfree

Christopher Ryne Winfree

My Sons

Clure Lancaster Winfree

Todd Ryne Winfree, 1959-1964

My Parents

CS and Frances Louise Winfree

My Family, Friends and Neighbors on Rawls Creek, TN.

Preface

This is a work of precious and unique memories. I have tried to write them truthfully. But I must acknowledge that a few may not be entirely pure and may be of events and people as I wish they had been. Everyone has that problem with memories. We subconsciously rearrange them a bit. It improves the taste. It is possible as well that some of my brother's stories have intruded and become part of my memories. That happens also with people and memories. But that could enhance my accuracy. So far as I can tell, Joe has never forgotten anything.

My sister, Jeraldine, is the opposite of Joe, and remembers nothing. My sister, Jean, claims to remember more than she possibly could. She was only a baby when we moved into the big world near Tucker's Cross Roads. I remember, however, that when I developed a minor, very minor, case of pimples during high school, she called me Bumps. It angered me.

I could not include everything in this book. Some examples of omissions may explain why they were omitted. I don't know why Trigger Mofield asked his sister to cut off his finger with an ax. I don't know why she did it. But I couldn't get much mileage out of saying, "Trigger Mofield's sister cut off his trigger finger with an ax," and that would be laughing at tragedy. I can't remember the name of the girl who helped me break into Fred Taylor Flippen's house and steal his Post Toasties. Anyway, I would be admitting a criminal act if I retold that story.

A strange event at the Rawls Creek School was the yearly attack on fellow student Howard Lester. All the boys and girls would whip up on poor Howard once a year right after school let out on a Friday afternoon. I do not know the leader of this event, but most everyone participated. We would pummel him to the ground and then pile onto him. The melee usually lasted four or five minutes, then was over for another year. Howard took it better than I could have, but I don't think he liked it. I don't remember why we did it.

While writing this book, I discovered that only a small pool of goodwill remains among my fellow graduates of Rawls Creek School. Faye Mofield spoke with me twice but did not want to add anything much to my memories. Chat Agee, living up to her name, chatted with me twice and was willing to talk more. I think she was mostly interested in forgetting rather than remembering. She, like Faye, could not remember the famed literary society that someone wrote about in a history of Smith County. If it existed, I didn't know, since I also don't remember it. Alma Mofield showed little interest in speaking with me. In fact she remained silent. Charles Preston is dead. Howard Lester did not return my calls.

Among the many differences noted in comparing life then and now, an inevitable result of dealing in memories, is the work ethic. That of the people who lived along Rawls Creek seems to be a relic of the past. They worked all day everyday from first light to well after dark. Daddy and Uncle Charlie preferred to run rather than walk. An example is when we hauled hay from the field to the barn. After the hay was raked and piled into what we called shocks, I drove the wagon pulled by a pair of mules between the rows of shocks. Daddy and Uncle Charlie ran along on either side and threw the hay into the wagon with pitchforks. Uncle Charlie always wanted me to get the mules moving at a fast pace so he and daddy could dash from shock to shock. If I didn't, I got covered up with hay. After the wagon was loaded, daddy and Uncle Charlie got aboard and we raced to the barn.

I would climb up into the loft and lower the big hay fork down from under the bonnet. It was fastened to a tow rope threaded through pulleys and out the back side of the barn where daddy had a mule to pull each fork load up from the wagon to the loft. I was privileged to move each batch to the interior of the loft and tramp it down. The temperature outside would be in the 90s. Inside, under a metal roof, it would be about 110 degrees. That, of course, was great fun.

Uncle Charlie finally worked himself to death while I was in the Army. I went home for the funeral. The rain had stopped a couple of days before, but the soil was still wet and sticky. At the cemetery I sat next to Uncle Tom as we watched two men shovel dirt onto Uncle Charlie. They worked slowly and with frequent breaks to clean their shovels with a shovel cleaning tool. I had never seen one before. Uncle Tom began to fidget and expel his breath noisily. At one of their breaks for shovel cleaning, he jumped up and grabbed both shovels while rudely pushing the men out of his way. He tossed one shovel to me and said, "Come on, James, and help me cover Charlie up. These people gonna take all day and Charlie will be spinning in the casket if he gets an idea what these bastards are doing. A shovel cleaning tool! Damn, what's wrong with the toes of their shoes? Always worked for me."

On another subject, it was a pleasure to work with my editor, William O. Bryant, and I wish to acknowledge his efforts and extend my appreciation. And a special thanks to my wife Rose, the lovely Woolly Bear as she is known, for all her interruptions, threats, snide remarks, and suggestions. As always she is the rock I lean on.

Contents

Chapter 1

Dust devils danced across the bare yard under the shade of the big hackberry trees and over the fence onto the dusty road. The fence posts shimmered in the blazing summer sun. Occasionally, a long, thin green snake slithered about in the upper branches of a hackberry, seeking an insect meal. Dr. Fisher's mare snorted at the swarm of gnats about her nose and swatted a horsefly with her tail. She was restless at being tied to a fence post for two hours in that heat. Pete, the mixed breed dog, lay curled under a privet bush, paws covering his nose. Pinkney and Mary Winfree sat with their son, CS, waiting for some word from inside the house.

Dr. Fisher finally stepped out onto the porch, shirt sleeves rolled up, wiping his face with a white towel, and announced, "Its a boy!" CS leaped to his feet and dashed toward the house, making the porch in one bound. Pinkney tugged at his chin whiskers and looked at Mary as she lifted her long black skirt and took the porch steps two at a time. Pinkney pulled a large railroad watch from his vest pocket and snapped open the cover. It was 1:00 p.m., August 24, 1932. Through some process, quite unknown to me at the time, involving a doctor, my mother, and my father, I was born. That day was an extremely hot one. Where did this momentous event occur? At the home of my mother and father on Rawls Creek in the 13th Civil District of Smith County, Tennessee.

Mama said I entered this world weighing approximately seven pounds, estimated because no scales were available other than those used for weighing grain and animal feed. I shall forever be grateful that daddy kept me out of the large grain bucket and from being suspended and balanced as if I were corn or wheat. My twenty-two-inch length was accurately measured, however, being ascertained by use of a sewing measurement tape. I have often wondered why the length of babies was so important to people in the South back in the '30s. Every parent could tell you how long the baby was when born, but few could give you the weight. Now I know it was because there was a scarcity of scales. No one wanted to take the new baby out to the barn and weigh it on the grain scales that were plentiful but only accurate to within a pound or so.

Seventy short years have passed since this occurrence, and Rawls Creek is still missing from most maps. Rawls Creek is a community along either side of the insignificant stream also called Rawls Creek. The community developed along the creek because the creek served as a road. It is for the most part the bottom of a valley between two rows of fairly small hills. The creek has a flat rock bottom and little water except for pools along occasional small bluffs.

The road in 1932 ran mostly in the creek bed except for the pools and bluffs, where it moved to the bank. In the few short miles, about three, of the road, it ran in and out of the creek twelve or fourteen times. It was a reasonably good dirt road until near Jesse Poston's house. There it went into the creek and largely stayed until it reached our house. Then it passed through a little canyon where a bridge later was built that allowed most traffic to cross. It was not much of a bridge, just a couple of big logs with some thick planks nailed across them. It served the purpose.

The first planks, placed two or three inches apart, made the bridge seem unsafe for horse or mule traffic. Horses and mules are not stupid. They will not go where there might be a chance to get a foot and leg caught between planks or in a hole. A sort of bypass across the creek and up the bank in front of our house allowed buggy and wagon traffic to go around the bridge. Later a new floor on the bridge, with planks closer together, allowed mules and horses to cross to a new road scratched out along the creek.

Wes and Ethal Dennis were regular every week in their buggy. I remember them as always well dressed. Miss. Ethal wore a blue dress with a white hat and Mr. Wes a dark suit, brown I think, with white shirt, tie, and a cream flat-topped straw hat. We called it a boater. Mr. Wes preferred to drive to Rock City to buy a few groceries rather than go to Grant, though they lived closer to Grant. Grant was a big town compared to Rock City. There were maybe thirty or forty people in Grant. Mr. Wes liked Julian Cooksey, who owned Cooksey's Store. We traded with Cecil Poston and Julian Cooksey in Rock City, and the peddler who came by in his big peddling wagon every week, on Thursday, I think.

Our house, built on the south side of the road beside a drive that had been the road before construction of the bridge, sat on the high side of the creek, eighty or ninety feet from the bridge. The road came out of the creek exactly in front of Wilson Marks' house. His house sat about a hundred or 150 feet above the road on the side of the hill across from our barn. Our barn almost touched the road.

We had a porch that ran the length of the front and the right side of the house. There were two fireplaces, one in each of the two rooms that opened onto the porch. My mother and father lived in the room on the left and my grandmother and grandfather (mammy and pappy) lived in the one on the right. A double chimney with a fireplace on either side separated the rooms. Behind the chimney was a small hall with a door at either end, providing an exit from each of the front rooms. The hallway only had three sides. The side opposite the chimney opened into a large dining room that was one step up from the hall. There was a kitchen on either end of the dining room. We used the one on the left. The one on the right belonged to my grandparents. The left end of the big table in the dinning room was ours and the right end was theirs. In later years other people found this arrangement odd. As far as I can remember it seemed perfectly normal to me.

We had no electricity, no indoor plumbing, no running water, no telephone, and no radio. Later Uncle Alton made me a radio out of a Kraft cheese box, copper wire, a crystal, a cat whisker, and a flat copper strip for a tuner. Daddy bought me a set of earphones to use with it. Pappy had a big radio that sometimes operated when the huge wet-cell battery produced enough power to make it run. At some point dry-cell batteries became available to us and we bought a new Philco.

*   *   *   *

Who Am I?

There was a large amount of confusion at the time of my birth, of which I was, quite naturally, totally unaware. No doubt my parents also were unaware. It appears that only Dr. J. E. Fisher was confused. I have no way of knowing except from what daddy and mama told me. You see, I only knew of the confusion years later when I enrolled, or tried to enroll, in the teaching program at Middle Tennessee State College. School officials quite foolishly insisted on being presented with some evidence of my birth. Any person of reasonable mental power easily could tell that I had been born by the obvious fact that I was there standing before them. But my mere presence was not enough for the highly educated people. They required paperwork attesting to the fact of my existence.

The more pompous of the men with whom I spoke insisted I travel to Nashville to the state office building. In the basement of that prestigious building, upon payment of one dollar, paperwork required to prove I existed would be forthcoming. I was in the office of the registrar at MTSC (now a university and thus MTSU) in Murfreesboro, Tennessee. I recently had arrived there by thumb, and had only the vaguest idea of the location of Nashville in relation to Murfreesboro. For that reason I returned to Lebanon, again using my thumb, then home, which by then was a different site from my birth.

When I explained the problem to my father (whose name really was CS), he volunteered to drive me to Nashville in the 1936 Chevrolet sedan that had seen us through WW ll. (We traded it later for a 1949 Chevrolet pickup truck.) In Nashville, on Charlotte Pike, in the midst of several large buildings near the state capitol, I jumped out to search for the paperwork required by MTSC. This also was where dad had bought all the leftover automobile license tags for 1933. That had been a very bad year for auto tag sales.

In the basement of the building, in a dusty, dank, and dark room, I located the bureau of vital statistics, or something similar to that. An extremely fat and unpleasant woman of indeterminate age, who appeared to have little or no interest in me, presided over the equally unpleasant room. The need of paperwork was plain to me because the fat woman did not notice me. No doubt she also did not believe I existed. The only paperwork I had with me was the dollar bill required. I waved it like a flag, thereby catching her attention.

"What do you want, a birth certificate?"

"Yes, ma'am," I replied.

"What's yore name and where and when were you born, yore father's name, and yore mother's name?'

I thought her knowledge of me remarkably lacking for someone who, for a dollar, was going to give me paperwork proving my existence. I answered as follows: "My name is James Lofton Winfree. I was born at home on August 24, 1932. My father's name is CS Winfree and my mother's name is Louise."

After much hunting through books and files and mumbling under her breath, she returned with some startling information. It seemed I was wrong. I actually did not exist, at least in the bureau of vital statistics.

"Here is what I've got, honey," she said. "CS Winfree and Mary Farnsworthy, on August 23, 1932, had a boy aptly named CS Winfree Jr. It is highly unlikely he and this Louise person had another the next day at the same time in the same place. You best check again to see who you are." She whisked the dollar out of my clinched fist, where it had been since the waving exercise. Then she produced a small sheet of paper, quickly stamped it with a rubber stamp, and placed her initials on it before handing it to me. I frankly admit I was chagrined, absolutely chagrined. (I've learned that word since then.) What could I do? I was only sixteen years old and had very little worldly experience. I got out of high school at an early age, but that did not mean I knew what to do in that situation. That unpleasant fat woman told me I did not exist, yet there I was. I decided to give the piece of paper to daddy, and let him sort it out.

My father was not prone to use much profanity. But I well remember the first time I heard him do so. It was early one morning in the barn when the temperature was in the low teens and it was snowing with some vigor. He and I were feeding and milking the cows. Daddy was trying to move one particularly obstinate cow to a more desirable position away from the stable wall by pushing her rump around. She did not seem to appreciate his efforts, and kicked rather vigorously backward with her right foot, striking him rather sharply in his privates. He said, "God damn you, you bitch," while holding her foot, caught as a reflex, which further irritated her. She kicked him again in about the same place, guided as it were by his own hands. Immediately after the second kick he dropped her foot and delivered a swift and vigorous kick of his own.

Although I was only about seven years old, I could have told him that was a mistake. He had on a pair of rubber boots that offered little or no protection for his feet, and provided no noticeable assistance to the kick. I have said before it was cold, and that is true. Bent over from the pain, he started hopping about on his non-kicking foot, and if I am not mistaken, he said, "Son of a bitch!" Leaning against the stable wall he began removing the boot and the sock, rather gingerly I might add. By then, though I was in a state of shock at his language, I could not help moving in close to see what was wrong with his foot. A glance revealed the sad spectacle. His feet were no doubt cold and the power of his kick to the cow mainly affected his dominant toe, the big one. The nail cracked as would a windowpane struck by a rock. I could tell it hurt. He replaced his boot without the sock, retrieved the milk bucket, and totally destroyed it against the offending cow's backside. I moved outside the barn quickly, and at a safe distance laughed quite heartily.

Another time I heard him use profanity was when I handed him the paper from the impolite fat woman. He looked at the paper for a time, then said to no one in particular, "Who the hell is Mary Farnsworthy?" I thought he ought to know.

Up to that moment I had not thought much about Mary Farnsworthy. I was wondering who the hell was CS Winfree Jr.? I don't recall that we ever figured out who Mary Farnsworthy was. We were pretty sure mother's name was Louise. And we were pretty sure my name was James Lofton Winfree.

*   *   *   *

Boys, I am writing this to you to try to explain the many changes made in this world since I was your age. I cannot envision the changes that will occur in the next seventy years. You may, when you reach my age, look back on even greater changes. I will not be here to see them and I can't even imagine them. But let me tell you about the 1930s and 1940s. Much of this is from my memories and does not pretend to be anything but memories of my life from August 24, 1932 to August 24, 1945. I am stopping at 1945 because that is the year I started to high school and also the year we moved to Wilson County. It is also the year I began to learn there is a world outside of the little world where I lived. It was the year World War II ended, and because of that it is an important year in my life.

*   *   *   *

The Great Automobile License Plate Purchase

I do not remember much of 1933, but it was extremely difficult for people in Smith County, Tennessee, and many other places. It was not a big success for the automobile license plate business. People either went without the plates or did not operate their autos. Many people did as daddy and Uncle Tom did. Daddy bought a set of plates and attached one to the rear of his car, and gave the other to Uncle Tom, who attached it to the rear of his car. They were careful not to park close to each other. The plates came two to a pack, one for the front and the other for the rear of the auto.

In 1936 my father went to Nashville and bought all the leftover boxes of unsold plates returned by the county court clerks across Middle Tennessee, or maybe the entire state. I do not know for sure. I do know he and Uncle Charlie made two trips to Nashville using two wagons per trip, each pulled by four mules. I think daddy paid $20.00 for the entire lot. The plates, packed in boxes containing fifty sets per box and weighing at least fifty pounds, were difficult to handle. After two trips there were still quite a number of boxes remaining. Tired of spending his time on a wagon back and forth to Nashville, Uncle Charlie refused to make another trip. Daddy agreed and they never went back for the balance.

My father was an ingenious man and knew exactly what he was going to do. We had several barns and outhouses and two regular houses that needed roofs. The license plates were perfect rectangles and made of heavy metal with a thick coat of enamel paint. They made perfect roofing shingles. They needed to have a slight bend, and we did this by pressing the plate across the thigh. This slight bend kept the plate snug against the roof decking when nailed in place. Mama and Aunt Florence bent the plates while Uncle Charlie and daddy nailed them to the deck or laths. The metal used to make the plate was so strong they had to hold the roofing nails with a pair of pliers and hit the nail a hefty blow to make it penetrate the plate. Then it was easy to drive the nails. It was after mashing his thumb and forefinger several times that daddy determined that pliers were the best way to proceed.

The private passenger car plates were dark brown with cream numbers. The taxi plates were green with white letters and numbers. We covered one of the houses with taxi plates, and they made an attractive roof. This very day one barn and maybe two of the out buildings are still standing and have the rusty auto license plates for a roof. There have been few or no leaks. License tags made good shingles.

*   *   *   *

Chapter 2

When I was about eight months old, maybe nine, I began to have earaches, which were painful. Upon hearing sudden screams and observing me poking a finger in my ear and pulling at the ear lobe, daddy diagnosed earache. No baby doctors existed anywhere near me. Maybe there were none anywhere in those days. The only doctors I ever knew were Dr. J. E. Fisher and Dr. Sloan. I don't remember his first name, if I ever knew it. Dr. Fisher gave us pills and Dr. Sloan dispensed liquids. Dr. Fisher said we should not have any truck with Sloan because he was a fraud who went around dissolving pills in water and selling his medicine at twice the price. So we never went to see Dr. Sloan or allowed him in our house. To this day I am suspicious of liquid medicine. Dr. Fisher had a horse and buggy and he also had a car, and he thought all good doctors went to see their patients. He did so whenever needed. This was another bone of contention between Dr. Fisher and Dr. Sloan, who was not much for getting out of his office. Oh, he did so from time to time, but it was his strong belief the sick needed to come into his office. Dr. Fisher was of the opinion that if you were able to get to the doctor's office, you were not very sick.

I later learned we had a rather large farm by the standards of the area and the time. There was another house on the farm about half a mile from where we were living, and then it was another quarter of a mile to the next farm. A wagon road ran from our house to the second house and on to the house where people lived on a farm owned by Melissa Highers. The woman there was sickly, actually very sickly, if her trips to see Dr. Sloan were any indication. When I say there was a wagon road, I am actually overstating the fact and improving on its actual condition. It took a very determined wagon driver to make that trip. Later my father improved the road until we could navigate it by auto. But that was later.

At the time of my story the road was barely passable, but that did not prevent the sickly woman from visiting Dr. Sloan on a regular monthly or oftener basis. I have thus far been unable to find anyone still living that knows that poor woman's name. Otherwise I would tell you. She rode a mule down to our house where sometimes she met Dr. Sloan, who transported her to his office in Carthage. Dr. Sloan usually resisted doing that, however, leaving it up to some of her relatives to perform the service. Normally this trip consumed the entire day, and often she remained somewhere overnight. We were aware of all her comings and goings because we had to look after her mule. We could not just leave the poor thing tied to a tree. Daddy would feed and water the old boy and put him on a rope of sufficient length to allow him access to water and grass, or in winter, hay.

From time to time someone representing Dr. Sloan, or occasionally the good doctor himself, would come to our gate to leave some medicine for this lady. Since we had no truck with Dr. Sloan or his liquid medicine, mama would give instructions that the bottles be left on the rock fence by the big hackberry tree. We assumed no responsibility for them and certainly would have none of the liquid quack medicine in our house. Often this arrangement was less than satisfactory to Dr. Sloan as the potions could freeze in winter weather. Mama suggested he take the medicine up the road to the sick woman's house if he did not want to leave it by the tree. The road, virtually impassable in summer, certainly was no better in winter, and Dr. Sloan or his representative would stand looking wistfully at the gate and the closed door to our house. Mama was not unfriendly, but as I have said, we had no truck with Dr. Sloan.

*   *   *   *

You boys may remember that when you were very young your mother took you to the pediatrician to get your shots. We did not have a pediatrician or any needle jabs, and for that reason I had no protection from all the common childhood diseases. Some of the maladies I had you probably have never even heard of in your young lives. By the time I was eight or ten years old, I had had measles, both red and German, mumps, chickenpox, assorted fevers, continuous sore throats, many earaches, and a broken nose. Had there been the shots of today I would have enjoyed the first seven years of my life much more.

Now back to my ear aches, which you both had and which were treated with drops, jabs and tubes. We had, as I have said, none of these. We did however have Hershel Mofield.

*   *   *   *

Hershel, The Traditional Healer

Hershel lived down the creek from us and was a frequent visitor, sometimes wanted and sometimes not. One of the advantages of Hershel was his habit of smoking. He smoked Golden Grain Tobacco that came in a white sack with a yellow label. Hershel commonly wore bib overalls, Wolverine work shoes with gray work socks, an old blue work shirt, and a floppy brown hat.

In the bib of his overalls Hershel kept his sack of Golden Grain and something you are, I hope, not at all familiar with, cigarette papers. The papers came in a little pack cut to size to roll around the tobacco and make a cigarette. Everyone would sit around Hershel and marvel while he rolled one of his coffin nails. The trick was in how he held the cigarette paper. Somehow he would use his first and second fingers and the thumb of his left hand to fold the cigarette paper into a U shape. With his right hand, he would remove the sack of Golden Grain from the bib pocket and open it, using his teeth to hold one of the strings that held the sack closed while he loosened the sack opening with the thumb and forefinger of the right hand. Once opened, he would fill the cigarette paper with tobacco, and reversing the procedure, re-close the sack and return it to his bib pocket. With a quick twist of the fingers of his left hand he would roll the paper into a tube, then lick the edge of one side of the paper and seal the roll. He now had a tube about two and one-half inches long filled with tobacco. After twisting both ends he would pop one end of the cigarette into his mouth, and striking a match on the leg of his overalls, light the other end. He would take a puff or two and blow smoke out both nostrils, amazing all of the young who watched.

One day while this event unfolded, I lay on my back crying and poking my right ear with a finger. It was time for Dr. Hershel to get to work. He sucked in a huge amount of smoke from the cigarette, leaned over me, and blew the smoke into my painful ear. After two or three puffs the pain in my ear went away. This treatment may seem strange to you but it was quite normal to me, and I might add, effective. Hershel did not charge for this treatment and gave neither pill nor liquid medicine to me, only warm tobacco smoke. We did not have any Blue Cross or any other type of insurance, nor did the government furnish us any. The government did not provide any service of any type on Rawls Creek, so far as I can recall.

* * * *

Rufus was a Republican

My daddy, like nearly all the people along the creek, in fact all of them except Rufus Highers, were Democrats and mostly liked the government because we had elected Franklin Delano Roosevelt, a Democrat, as President. People would point at Rufus with the first finger of the right hand and giggle behind their left hands, which covered their mouths. They snickered, "He's a Republican!"

Rufus had the newest car on the creek, but that did not count for much because it was a Plymouth. The Democrats on the creek were Ford and Chevrolet people. We were Ford people until 1939, when we switched to the 1936 Chevrolet, and my father remained that way. Owning a Plymouth and being a Republican were like having a communicable disease.

Rufus was strange in another way. He had an outlook on life not subscribed to by his neighbors. Rufus said on numerous occasions, "If I can live to be 50, I will be ready to die and get out of the way." This view of Rufus' caused his neighbors to shake their heads. A Republican with a Plymouth who wanted to die when he became 50 was incomprehensible. My Uncle Tom certainly did not subscribe to that philosophy.

One of the few times Aunt Ocie got Uncle Tom to go to church with her he embarrassed her to such a degree she waited several months, maybe a year, before she began to prod him about church again. It seems the service was one of dedication and renewal that Uncle Tom no doubt needed. The preacher, an evangelist of the fire and brimstone persuasion, gave a rousing sermon, bringing more than one of the good sisters to the brink of shouting and swooning. This was apt to occur at a renewal and rededication service. At the end of his diatribe the preacher exhorted all the worshippers who wanted to go to heaven to come to the front of the church and stand. After several calls, the entire congregation was standing in front of the preacher except Uncle Tom. The preacher raised both hands skyward and looked at Uncle Tom through his unblinking eyes and asked in his thunderous voice, "Don't you want to go to heaven, Tom?"

Uncle Tom, no shrinking violet himself, responded in an equally thunderous voice, "Shore I want to go to heaven, but I didn't know you were getting up a load tonight."

An almighty hush fell over the crowd. The would-be heaven travelers began to go back to their seats. The preacher said a brief prayer and Aunt Ocie took Uncle Tom home. Unlike Rufus, Uncle Tom was in no hurry to wind up his earthly affairs. It upset no one when Rufus moved to Detroit, probably because almost everyone shared Uncle Tom's views. Rumor has it that the preacher did not pray for Uncle Tom.

*   *   *   *

Uncle Tom was a Trader

Uncle Tom, a farmer and a trader, was known as a "pin hooker," a term for men who made on offer on most anything found for sale. He also was willing to sell almost anything he owned, if the price was right. Sometimes he even sold things he didn't own.

Once at the stockyards in Lebanon, I was standing next to Uncle Tom, leaning against a truck loaded with cattle, when another pin hooker came by and looked at the cattle for several minutes. He scratched his chin several times and shook his head as if something bad had just occurred. He sidled up next to Uncle Tom and took out a bag of RJR smoking tobacco. He rolled a cigarette while continuing to shake his head. With the unlit cigarette hanging out of the corner of his mouth, he said, "Too bad about this market. Cattle ain't bringing nothing."

"Is that right?" Uncle Tom answered as if he didn't care one way or the other: I don't think he did.

"You have any idea what those cows will bring in there? Got a little age on them, haven't they?"

"Uh huh." Uncle Tom sort of muttered his answer.

"You want to sell them?"

"That is why they are in this sale line. Don't many people bring cows here for practice." I liked it when Uncle Tom was trading. He pulled out his pocket watch and looked at the time. "I been here almost three hours and haven't had any lunch and no beer. Place is too damn slow. I may just go home."

"Don't do that, mister. I will buy them cows and take them off your truck and then you can go home," the pin hooker said in a way that made me think he really wanted to buy those cows. "I'll pay you eleven hundred and thirty-five dollars cash. You sign my bill of sale and I will hand you the money." As he said this he dragged a big wad of money from his hip pocket.

I thought Uncle Tom was going to punch him. "Hell's the matter with you? Shit, I thought you said you wanted to buy them, not steal them. Just get on out of here." Uncle Tom said "Shit" again.

The pin hooker jerked back, rolled his eyes toward the sky, extracted a match from the pocket in his bib overalls, and scratched it with a dirty thumbnail until a flame sprang to life. He looked at the flame for a long moment, then lit the cigarette hanging from the corner of his mouth. He sucked and puffed until he had a good smoke fog about his head before saying anything more to Uncle Tom.

"You ain't been inside have you? If you knew what stock is bringing in there you'd know I made you a fair offer. I probably lose money after the sale costs are paid."

Uncle Tom said, "Shit."

"Them's old cows. You know old cows are just canners and cutters. Won't bring nothing." The pin hooker rubbed his left eye with the knuckle of his right index finger. Smoke got into it most likely.

"You want these cows they'll cost you fourteen hundred and fifty dollars," Uncle Tom said.

The pin hooker figured it was his turn, so he also said, "Shit."

Uncle Tom looked at me and made a move toward the sale barn. I followed. The pin hooker sort of pawed the ground with the toe of a size thirteen Wolverine shoe. Just as I passed by him the pin hooker yelled at Uncle Tom.

"Wait a minute, feller. I'll tell you my final offer. I pay you thirteen hundred even for them cows. That's it. Not another penny."

"Where's your bill of sale you want me to sign?"

Uncle Tom sold him the cows, then looked at me as he pocketed the money. "Come on, James, we got to go."

As we long-legged it across the lot I inquired where we had to go. Uncle Tom explained to me the need to find the fellow who owned the cows he had just sold and see if we could buy them for about eleven hundred bucks.

*   *   *   *

Chapter 3

D. Poston came into my life in late 1934 when I was a bit over two years old. D. was a truck driver, road builder, cattle hauler, excavator, jack-of-all-trades, and my best friend for several years. He had a huge Ford truck suitable for all-purpose work, and it was in constant use. I helped him build lots of roads through the other creek that ran through our farm. It was an unnamed stream but an important one for our farm. D. wore "Stevens Shirts & Pants that Match." His were tan-colored, long-sleeved shirts buttoned at the neck, and pants with cuffs. He would not wear Wolverine shoes for he knew that mule leather leaks. Any fool knew mule skin had big pores and shoes made out of mule leather would leak like a fish net. D. wore high-top shoes made from the best horse leather, with rawhide laces. In the summer he wore a straw hat with three eyelets in either side of the crown for ventilation. In winter he had a fine leather cap with a short bill buttoned to the top edge. Today we call it a driving cap or a beret. I always called it D.'s fine leather cap.

D.'s hair was black and curly, not the scraggly red hair that was the trademark of most of the Postons. Nor were his face and arms splotched with the freckles that went with the other Postons' red hair. D. and I got on very well, for we were both strong, hardworking, and handsome, even though I was just a kid. I remember once we were taking a load of cows to the livestock sale when several of them fell off the truck. D. jumped out, rounded up the cows, and got them back on the truck. They brought a good price that made daddy happy. Once we built a road from Rock City to Grant to get the road out of the creek. D. never had to drive in the creek again. D. and I worked together until I started to school. Then he went away and I never saw him again. For some reason I never missed him.

*   *   *   *

I want you boys to look back to 1935 when I was three years old, the same age as Christopher as I write this, and compare the world I lived in then with the world you lived in at the same age. At age three, I had never been to Nashville, or even to Lebanon, about twenty miles from where I lived. I had been to Carthage, probably ten miles away. By that age you were world travelers compared to me. I am not sure you have been to Lebanon or Carthage, but you have been to Nashville, Memphis, Knoxville, Atlanta, Orlando, Denver, and points between. Not only have you been to those and other places, you in many instances flew in an airplane. I, on the other hand, had never seen an airplane. I did not even know there were airplanes.

*   *   *   *

Chapter 4

During Christmas of 1935, John Steelman and his son, Robert, came to see daddy. John was a "sharecropper." That meant that he put in a crop on someone else's land and took it all the way to sale for a share of the sale price, usually fifty percent. He proposed to put in one of daddy's tobacco crops since daddy had two farms. This, he opined, would be of benefit to daddy since pappy was old and sickly and not able to put in a crop anymore. John made his case by insulting me. He indicated I was too little to be of any help. He also made a big deal about mama not being of any help because she would have another baby to look after by summer. This bit of news sort of stunned me, but everyone seemed uninterested in my inquiries on that subject. It turned out John Steelman knew what he was talking about, for Dr. Fisher came on the next June 22, and when he left, I had a sister, Geraldine.

John said Robert would be of help to him because he was older and bigger than me. I think Robert was about six or seven years old and weighed around 40 pounds. I figured D. Poston and I could work circles around both the Steelmans. But daddy made a deal with John and he and Robert made plans for a big tobacco crop.

*　　　*　　　*　　　*

Preparing the Plant Bed

Raising tobacco was no easy chore. Daddy said you needed a year that was thirteen months long to grow good tobacco. A plot for the plant bed, selected at least by early spring and carefully prepared, got the crop off to a good start. The plants, called slips, grown to transplant size in the plant bed, provided the second step in the thirteen-month crop process. We had to plow, chop, and otherwise make ready the selected site to receive the tobacco seed. A plant bed was about six feet wide and forty or fifty feet long. Some farmers made a double bed, but not daddy. He preferred a long single bed. If he had decided to make a double bed it would have been twelve or fourteen feet wide. The number of slips needed to set out in the patch determined the size of the plant bed. The size of the patch determined the number of slips required.

Having decided how big the bed was to be, we cut poles to make the sides of the bed, then stacked and set aside the poles until after burning off the bed. Next, we piled the brush on the prepared bed site to a height of at least five feet and a foot or so wider than the finished bed. All the limbs and branches cut from the poles, which were actually fairly large saplings, were used on the brush pile. Most tobacco farmers mixed at least fifty percent dry brush and limbs with the green limbs and brush to produce a good fire. For this reason many farmers saved the limbs and brush when they cut a supply of winter firewood during the fall. This gave the brush time to dry out until burning in March or April. The purpose of burning off the plant bed was to kill the weed seed in the ground. The purpose of the bed was to grow tobacco slips and not weeds, hence the burning. The bed needed to burn for several hours to make sure of cooking all the seeds possible. Usually the neighbors made a community party out of burning the plant bed. The women all came to the house and prepared dinner and supper. The men stood around talking, telling tales, smoking, chewing, spitting, and occasionally stoking the fire. I do not doubt some of the men took a little nip on occasion. I suspect this occurred when, from time to time, they were damning the Germans for their transgressions.

Burning a plant bed was nowhere near as important an event as wheat thrashing. Everyone came to a wheat thrashing. The owner of the thrashing machine brought it into each community and set up, staying for a few days, or until all the wheat in the surrounding area was thrashed. On Rawls Creek, they often put the thrasher on our farm because we had an easily accessible and level site and a lot of wheat. Every other year the wheat thrashing was at May Poston's place farther up the creek. It was not as happy an event then. May Poston did not open his house to the thrashers and farm families. It was a bring-your-own-lunch event and not very popular. But every year there also was a thrashing at Horace Flippen's farm. The thrasher crew loved that because Mrs. Irene put on the best dinner anywhere. She had a dining room with a big round table that seated ten people if they crowded up a bit. She had three sittings. First table was all men, second table women and boys old enough to help with the thrashing work, and third table was for children. I moved to the men's table the last year we lived on the creek.

The women always helped Mrs. Irene with dinner. Usually Aunt Florence, mama, and Mrs. Lillie May were the regulars. Of course, Mary Alice and others of the older school girls helped. They would fill the table completely with bowls and platters full of vegetables and meat. Once the plates and iced tea glasses were on the table there was no room for anything else. While the big platters and bowls of food were off the table and in the hands of the diners, passing from one to the other, Mrs. Irene always eased an extra bowl or two onto the table. The women grinned and watched to see who ended up with a bowl or platter with no place to put it. Sometimes one of the men would end up with a bowl in each hand. It was an old familiar game and all the men pretended not to notice the man with the extra serving dishes. The women thought it great fun. The plant bed burning dinners were fun, but not comparable to wheat thrashing meals.

After the fire had burned itself out and the ashes cooled, we removed the pieces of wood that did not burn completely and worked the ashes into the soil with hoes and spades. We raked and smoothed the bed. Then we took the poles from the stack and placed them around the bed in a nearly perfect rectangle. We sowed the tobacco seed and covered the bed with canvas, which came in rolls of either six or eight-foot widths. The canvas was a fine mesh made of a strong fiber. It protected the bed from damage caused by heavy rains before the seeds had time to sprout. It also protected the tender slips from being burned by the strong rays of the sun.

*   *   *   *

Pegging It Out

When the slips reached the desired size, the next process, called "pegging them out," started in the field (patch) where the tobacco grew until cutting time. The patch required lots of preparation before planting the slips. Daddy plowed and disked his patch and laid it off in rows. The patch was perfect before he found it acceptable for planting, all the clods busted and the rows straight.

Near the middle of April, the slips were ten to twelve inches tall and ready to move to the patch when we got a good rain. We did not want to set the slips out in dry soil and water them by hand. We really looked forward to mud. John Steelman and Robert helped us set out our patch and we helped them set out theirs. That was the way farmers worked. Aunt Florence and Uncle Charlie helped us, so did J.R. Mofield and Marcellus.

This was hard, dirty work. It required two people. One carried the slips and dropped one every step down the rows that daddy laid out. Uncle Alton dropped the slips. He took over mama's job because she had gotten big with child and tired easily. The second man had a peg about two inches in diameter and twelve inches long. He straddled the row, bent over, and made a hole with the peg beside each slip. Next he placed the slip in the hole, and using the peg, pushed soil tightly around the roots. When daddy was pegging he never looked up or stood up until he reached the end or the row. The pegging out was a source of competition for everyone. They raced to the end of the row, then stood up, stretched, and went at it again, going back the other way. That year I was too small to help. I was sorry because I wanted to help. Five years later I was just the right size, and after the first day I wished I were a baby again.

After this there was nothing but work with the tobacco until time to start over again. First, we replanted any slips that died or got broken off by chickens, or ground hogs, or whatever might have gotten over, through, or under the fence. Then we hoed until the plants grew to plowing size. Then we plowed and plowed every week to keep the weeds out of the patch. Also we hoed and chopped the particularly aggressive weeds that avoided the plow. Then came the tobacco worms we had to pick off the plants and kill. Daddy toted a big bucket with half a gallon of coal oil in it. He put the worms in the coal oil to kill them.

When the tobacco plants reached a height of five or six feet it was time to top them. Cutting the top out stops the plant from growing tall and going to seed. Going to seed is when the plant diverts all its strength to developing seed to preserve its species. We did not need seed, and if we did two or three plants left with tops would make enough seed to plant Georgia. Also, topping the plant sends to the leaves the strength that would have gone to the seed and produces bigger and better tobacco leaves.

*   *   *   *

Suckers Suckering

When the plants were big we had another problem brought on by the topping. The leaves could not absorb all the nutrients, so sprouts developed where the leaves grew out from the stalk. Sprouts, called suckers, were no good for anything but wasting nutrients, so we cut them out with a sharp knife. Suckering was a dirty word to young farm boys. At suckering time the plants were so big the leaves touched each other across the rows and between plants. Most of the boys assigned to sucker were no taller than the tobacco plants, so all day tobacco leaves wiped across your face as you reached for a sucker. The leaves were gummy and bitter, with occasional worms, wasps, grasshoppers, and God knows what else, wiping across your face, mouth, and eyes. When the day ended, a boy who had suckered all day was a mess. John Steelman would look at Robert and say, "I think I will just throw him away. It'll be easier to have another one than it'll be to clean this'n up." Robert was not amused.

Going between the rows to cut out the suckers was tedious work and we had to do it very carefully. The leaves were money, and a leaf broken off was money thrown away. Once, while suckering, daddy noticed the return of the worms. He despaired of picking off the worms. In an empty twelve-pound flour sack, daddy put five pounds of powdered arsenic of lead, a good poison. Back in the patch, he shook arsenic of lead over the plants and worms. Hungry little buggers ate the lead and died and fell off to the ground. A sad side effect was that birds ate the fat worms and died also. When finished, daddy was white all over from the arsenic of lead he had dusted over an acre of tobacco plants.

When I became old enough and big enough to help dust the tobacco, I became as covered with the white arsenic of lead as daddy. Daddy always ran down to the deep spot in the creek and dunked himself, clothes and all, until the water washed the arsenic away. I always joined him, with or without arsenic of lead. The water felt good. I wondered how the minnows (there were no fish in Rawls Creek) got on with the arsenic of lead. I often wondered if the tobacco companies washed the tobacco well before making it into plugs and twists for chewing or cigarettes for smoking. Daddy never touched the stuff, so he did not worry about that sort of thing.

*   *   *   *

Cut it, Spike it, Hang it, and Let it Cure

The last dusting completed, the last sucker cut, the tobacco, a nice yellow color, was ripe for harvesting. Now we had to cut it, spike it on tobacco sticks, and hang it in the tobacco barn to dry. Our tobacco sticks were about five feet long and maybe one and one half inches on a side. They were hand split out of tough wood. The spike was a steel cone with a base large enough to fit over the end of a tobacco stick and tapered to a sharp point. The spike was about twelve inches in length. Daddy and Uncle Charlie cut the tobacco by working together. From time to time they alternated jobs. Daddy cut for a while and Uncle Charlie spiked, then they switched.

The way to do it was to shove a stick into the ground far enough for it to stand up unaided. The spike was placed over the end of the stick. Daddy, right-handed, held it with his left hand and took a stalk of tobacco from Uncle Charlie and spiked it onto the stake about a foot from the cut end. A cut stalk of tobacco was approximately four and a half feet in length and a stake would hold five stalks. Daddy could tell when they had cut enough tobacco for the day. Usually this occurred near lunch time.

Tobacco ready for cutting was gummy, sticky, smelly, and heavy. This meant that by noon the men were sticky, smelly, dirty, and tired. Noon in late August was hot with the temperature in the 90s and rising. After dinner (At noon we ate dinner, in the evening we ate supper. Lunch was something we took to school to eat at dinner.) we hitched the mules up to the wagon and hauled the cut tobacco to the tobacco barn.

Our tobacco barn was four-tiers high. That means it had four levels of tier-poles on which to hang the tobacco to dry, or cure. The tier-poles were the proper distance apart to hang the tobacco without crowding. The levels of tier-poles were roughly five feet apart. We needed four people to unload the wagon and hang the tobacco. One person stood on the poles making up the fist tier, and took a stick of tobacco from the person on the wagon. He handed it up to the person standing on tier two, who passed it up to the person on tier three. That person lifted it above his head and hung it on tier four.

That was hard work and fraught with danger. When you stood on the tier-poles it was with your left foot on one pole and your right foot on another pole that was at least four feet from the one under your left foot. Long legs were helpful. Short legs meant you had to be on the wagon or hang the tobacco just on the first tier. Every year we heard about a farmer falling from the top tier in his barn and breaking bones. Daddy worked the top tier and did not fall. Uncle Charlie was too big and heavy for the top tier.

*   *   *   *

I am going to digress here and tell you about something I just remembered about Uncle Charlie. I may have mentioned he was tight with his money. When I was in the seventh or eighth grade in school we went to the fair in Alexandria. That was the biggest and best fair near us, and we liked to go. There was mama, daddy, Geraldine, Joe, Aunt Florence, Uncle Charlie, and me. I think it cost about twenty-five cents to get into the fairgrounds. The sign read "Children Six and Under Get In Free." Uncle Charlie lifted me up in his arms and said to the dour-faced ticket-taker, "This'n is big for his age but he ain't quite seven yet," and walked in. I looked over his shoulder and saw a whole raft of big-for-their-age, not-quite-seven-yet, kids being lifted up by a dad or an uncle as they neared the ticket-taker.

*   *   *   *

Dry, Cure, Strip, Grade, and Sell

The tobacco hung in the barn and air-dried and cured. That process took about two months, so by the first or middle of November it was ready to be stripped, graded, and readied for sale. The tobacco now was dry and brittle and could not be handled until it came "in order." That term stemmed from the fact that the leaves had to no longer be dry and brittle before they could be stripped from the stalk. This condition came about when the weather became damp in November or December. The hot, dry air of summer drained all the moisture from the tobacco leaves, and the dry leaves then absorbed the humid air of autumn and became soft and pliable. The tobacco was "in order." Some farmers referred to that condition as being "in case." They said that meant in case they were ready to strip and grade the tobacco it was also.

Stripping the tobacco was simply stripping the leaves off the stalk. As I remember, four grades per stalk was par. The bottom few leaves were the lugs, good tobacco but ragged at the edges. The next few leaves were bright, the best on the stalk, followed by the reds. Reds might make up the rest of the leaves on a stalk, but quite often there were a few leaves left, called tips. Not quite good enough or big enough for reds, they would hurt the price of the reds if you tried to slip them in. Each person only stripped one grade and I usually got the tips. Hard to mess up all that's left, daddy said.

Most people stripped the tobacco off the stalk with their left hand. They held the leaves evenly by the stem end until they accumulated a hand full, then tied the stalk ends together with a tobacco leaf.

Interestingly this was called a hand. Stripping the leaves with the left hand made it possible to tie the stalks together with the right hand.

We stripped, graded, and piled the tobacco in stacks by grade, and covered it with tarps or sacks to keep it "in order." Then we took it to the tobacco sales warehouse in Carthage. We used wagons pulled by our fine team of mules. We did not have a truck.

At the warehouse we placed the tobacco on baskets furnished for that purpose by the warehouse. I don't remember how much we put on each basket, but the warehousemen weighed them and tagged each basket with our name, grade, and the weight. Usually there were three or four tobacco company employees who inspected each basket, or spot-checked the baskets. They scribbled something on a tag and added it to the basket. Daddy said they made notes helpful to the buyer from their company.

Three days later the buyers arrived and we returned to Carthage to watch the sale and get our money. The auctioneer went down the rows of baskets at a fast walk, chanting whatever it was he chanted. The only thing I understood was that every so often he said, "Sold American." I hoped it was ours they bought.

The buyers all had walking sticks, and from time to time they punched a basket and signaled with the stick, and a warehouseman would drag that basket out of the line to reweigh. First he made the farmer rearrange the tobacco and remove the rocks he has mixed in with the tobacco to make it weigh more. The buyers weren't dumb. They knew what tobacco weighed.

*   *   *   *

Chapter 5

I believe my memories actually became mine in 1937 and not memories of incidents I heard from others. I believe I remember things from when I was born, but others doubt that. I do remember 1937. It was a memorable year for me.

*   *   *   *

It is the 24th day of August 1937, and it is my fifth birthday. I have a new little sister, now about a year old. Her name is Geraldine. At this point I must digress again (I also learned that word later) and point out that some years later Geraldine changed the spelling of her name to Jeraldine. This is due to the continuing stream of brothers and sisters my mother and father produced, i.e., Joe, Jean, Judy and Jan, to go along with my James.

*   *   *   *

Now back to Geraldine, a hopelessly irritable baby determined to allow no one a good night of sleep or much rest during the day. And then there was me, requiring some attention and time. Fortunately for my mother, I was intelligent and she saw a way to ease her days by ridding herself of me and only having to deal with Geraldine, who must sleep at some time. This she did in the afternoons.

Too smart for my own good

My mother pointed out to my father that school began the following week and reminded him of my superior intelligence. She suggested it was time I be sent to school. Tired from work in the fields and also suffering lack of sleep, he was quick to see the validity of her reasoning.

Thus, on or about the 30th day of August 1937, I walked the one mile-plus to the Rawls Creek Elementary school. The teacher, Mrs. Gladys House, greeted me at the door with some trepidation and disappointment. That year she had no one else in the first grade. There were eight in the second grade. What was she to do with a first grader? His father was a prominent farmer and a justice of the peace. The latter made him also a member of the county court with lots of clout with the school board. The thought went through her mind to send the boy home for another year. As quickly as it came, the thought departed. She welcomed me into the one-room schoolhouse, showed me to my desk, and told me where to put my lunch of river bread, sausage, and biscuit. "This," she told the other pupils, "is James Winfree. For the first month he will do the primer and the next month he will do the first grade. Then he will join the second grade. Say hello to James, class." They did. I was with them for the next seven years. On my first day there were twenty-seven of us divided over the eight grades and the primer, which you call kindergarten today.

I watched the second grade group as they recited and knew that soon I would be one of them. They were Mary Catherine, Chat Agee, Alma Mofield, Fay Lee Mofield, Howard Lester, and Charles Preston.

I stood by my newly assigned desk and looked about the room in amazement. The room had eight rows of desks with six desks in each row, lined up two desks against the left wall as you stood in the entrance. Then there was an aisle for the teacher to walk among the students, two more desks, another aisle, and the last two desks. There was another aisle between those desks and the wall on the right side. This wall had a long plank nailed to it, four feet above and parallel to the floor. It had twenty-penny nails driven into it every foot or so, leaving about half of each nail sticking out for hanging coats. The opposite wall included windows low enough for me to see out when standing, but too high to see out when seated at my desk. This was to keep us from being distracted by events outside, yet letting in light for us to study by. But nothing went on outside except for an occasional cow that wandered by.

On either side of the entrance door hung two large blackboards with bottom rails for chalk and erasers. The teacher's desk was on a stage, or platform, ten or twelve inches higher than the classroom floor. That was where the pupils came to recite their lessons. There was also a blackboard on the wall behind the teacher's desk that reached all the way over to the window wall. The stage ended ten feet from the wall with the coat racks and had a rear door opening onto a porch. The porch held the wood for the big pot-bellied stove near the rear door.

The size of this room astounded me. It was bigger than my house and my house was a large house. On the creek only May Poston and Melissa Highers had bigger houses than ours. I was unaware of houses anywhere else. Actually, I was unaware of anywhere else.

It was evident that the next two or three months were going to be difficult for me. I suffered pangs of fear that were almost panic. I dreaded when the time came for the primer and first grade to recite and cipher. It was just the teacher and me on the stage with all the other classes looking at me. I ached to join the second grade.

*   *   *   *

Looking back sixty years later, I can not say my first day at school was much of a success. All the boys laughed at me because I was so small. And when I went into the boy's outhouse, John M. Mofield and Charles Preston shook it until I was too scared even to do Number 1. No way would I ever attempt Number 2. The girls mostly ignored me. However, the children treated me respectfully because I was Mr. CS's' boy, and that was important.

Before I forget, let me tell you about the big event of 1938. I believe it was in April. Already I was in the second grade and reciting and ciphering with the best.

*   *   *   *

Bill Monroe Was A Good Man

Mrs. Gladys announced that a big event would be coming the next week. Bill Monroe and the Blue Grass Boys would be performing at the schoolhouse. Admission would be ten cents for adults and five cents for children of school age. Wow! My mind boggled. I had never seen anyone from the Grand Ole Opry, but I had heard them on my crystal radio set. I hoped my daddy had a quarter so we could go. There would be no charge for Geraldine as she was not school age. If she cried as usual, they might pay her to leave.

Daddy had a quarter and we all went to the big show in our T-Model Ford. Daddy had on his clean and freshly starched overalls, the good ones with galluses that snapped fore and aft, not the high-backed ones that snapped only fore and caused great problems when attempting Number 2. I hated high-backs. Also, his were the real Duck Heads that "wear like iron." He was wearing a white shirt buttoned at the neck, and his fine leather cap.

I had on my new boots that laced up to my knees with a pouch for my knife on the right boot. The pouch contained a real Tree Brand knife. Class! My mother had on an old dress that was damage proof if Geraldine threw up all over her, which she did frequently. The schoolhouse filled to standing room only.

We had seats on the first row in chairs set up especially for us. Daddy, as I said, had a lot of clout with the school board that approved use of the schoolhouse for the Bill Monroe show. Bill Monroe sang a lot of songs, including the "Mule Skinner Blues." I did not know why anyone wanted to be a mule skinner. Everyone knew mule hide was not worth anything except to make Wolverine shoes. Mule hide leaks like a sieve.

Before the show started Bill Monroe was standing by the door, greeting the people and supervising the collection of the money. He spotted my friend Joe Kinslow standing back behind the line of people with a sad look on his broad, homely face. Barefoot and wearing only a ragged pair of high-back overalls, and in need of a haircut, Joe appeared dejected. I still remember the look on Joe's face, and it affects me yet. Bill Monroe walked over to Joe with a smile on his face. "What is your problem, son? This is no place for someone looking sad."

"I only have three pennies," Joe said with tears running down his dirty cheeks.

Bill Monroe patted Joe's head with his left hand, and with a smile as big as the world, looked Joe in his teary eyes and said, "That is all you need, son. Go over and give it to that lady with the cigar box and find yourself a place. I appreciate you coming."

Joe was a new and elated person with a hero for life.

*   *   *   *

Duty, the Pet Chicken

Geraldine had this strange and hypnotic ability to train chickens and make them into pets. The one I remember most she named Duty. I do not know why. This chicken led a happy and charmed life for a few months. Duty never strayed far from Geraldine, a habit she, like the other pet chickens, soon came to regret.

Geraldine managed to start training her chickens to be pets shortly after they hatched. Duty's mother was what we called an old dominicker hen. (OK, I know that may not be the correct spelling but it gets the meaning across.) I suppose Duty would have become an old dominicker hen if she had resisted being Geraldine's pet.

They were inseparable. That chicken was like an ankle bracelet. Geraldine would feed Duty from the palm of her hand and give her water the same way. Joe Kinslow and I shook our heads in disgust. Why would anyone want a chicken for a pet? A chicken is nothing like a dog or a cat, since they are capable of showing affection and concern. They can also be housebroken. I don't think you can housebreak a chicken. Duty certainly showed no signs of being housebroken. That dumb chicken would do Number 2 whenever she wanted and do it wherever she happened to be when the urge struck her.

Our mother would not let her into the house. She wouldn't even let our dog, Pete, in the door, and no one had ever seen him take a crap. Pee on the persimmon tree maybe, but Number 2 was not a spectator event for Pete.

One hot summer afternoon Duty became the first victim of Geraldine's clumsy love. While expressing attachment to her owner, Duty was accidentally stepped on by Geraldine. Oh, it was a sad scene: Duty squashed, Geraldine screaming at the top of her shrill voice, Pete licking his lips at, he presumed, a fine snack.

After Duty, there was a string of seven, perhaps eight, repeats of this tragedy. The carnage took place over a period of two or three years. Mama marveled at the gullibility and stupidity of chickens. Only Corine, another of Geraldine's pet hens, survived the chicken squashings.

*   *   *   *

Chapter 6

I am sure you are familiar with the phenomenon of aurora borealis. However, when I was your age it was a complete mystery to me. Aurora borealis is, according to Webster's *New World Dictionary*, luminous bands, or streamers, of light sometimes appearing in the night sky of the northern hemisphere, believed to be electrical discharges in the ionized air. Aurora borealis is also called northern lights.

I was about six years old when daddy called me to come out into the front yard. We had no back yard. He wanted me to look at the sky. The entire night sky was afire. It was full of red, orange, purple, and yellow lights, with some tinges of green, all moving in beautiful, intricate, and ever-changing patterns and colors. "Is the sky on fire?" I asked. Daddy said no, but mama had a different opinion. She was sure the world was coming to an end. Mammy agreed with mama. We watched the sky in some amazement and awe. Pretty soon Wilse Marks showed up about three sheets in the wind, and sided with mammy and mama.

I saw J.R. Mofield and Marcellus and Clifton coming up the road to our house. They carried an unlit lantern. Though it was usually dark at that time of day, requiring a lantern to see where you were walking, the sky was bright enough that they didn't need the lantern. They came to ask my father if this was the northern lights or if part of the world was on fire. They had seen, at least J.R. had seen, the northern lights before, but tonight they were so bright he agreed with mammy and mama. Daddy spoke quietly to keep down panic when Aunt Babe and Uncle Sam came running up in near hysteria. "The world is coming to an end," Aunt Babe announced. Amazingly, during all of this excitement, Geraldine remained asleep. Daddy suggested we move farther up the road to get a better view, but I knew he was moving us away from the house so we wouldn't awaken Geraldine.

I was aware the folks on the creek regarded my daddy as a special person. I wasn't exactly sure of why. Then I saw all the people arriving to consult with him about the fire in the sky. A.J. Mofield and his wife and a couple of his boys, Albert and Julian, came down the road, followed by Fred Taylor Flippen and Uncle Charlie and Aunt Florence. I knew that before the night ended most of the community would be in our yard looking at the great northern lights and being reassured by daddy.

Now it is sixty years later and I have seldom seen the northern lights since that first time. Today we live in a world so light at night, or so smoggy, that the northern lights are only a memory for most of us. It is a shame that little boys and girls can't go out into their yards and get to see the northern lights every two or three years.

*   *   *   *

Churns, Germans, and High-Back Overalls

On both sides of the road near our barn trees grew in mass. Elm trees (the blight had not emerged to attack the elms in those days), oak, hackberry, cedars, mulberry, and locust all grew together, giving shade all over the road for two hundred or three hundred yards, all the way from our house to the Kinslow house. Our mail box and the Marks' mailbox were side by side under two mulberry trees on the north side of the road, on the south bank of Rawls Creek just before the bridge. Directly across the road from the mailboxes, Wilse Marks placed two large rocks beside each other. The rocks were next to where daddy put the milk cans on Tuesday and Friday, when the milkman picked them up. They were the big ten-gallon size; the milk cans, not the rocks.

We had twenty-two Jersey milk cows and one Holstein. We milked them twice daily. I was not very good at milking, so daddy did most of it. Sometimes mama helped him. We used big stainless steel milk buckets that held three gallons of milk. When the buckets were full, we took them to the barn. There we strained out any foreign matter such as flies, straw, cow hairs, and the like. Then we poured the strained milk into the big gal-vanized milk cans. The milk we kept for our personal use we put in jars and stored in the cellar where it was cool. If mama needed to make butter, she put milk in the separator to let the cream rise to the top. Then she drained off the skim milk from the bottom and churned butter from the cream.

Ours was a really good churn. It was a crock churn, brown on the top third and white on the bottom two-thirds. Daddy made a wooden lid for it with a hole in the center for the dasher handle to go through. The dasher consisted of two wooden strips fastened together in the shape of a plus sign or a cross. The handle fastened to the cross and, in our case, was a three-foot piece cut out of a broom handle. It went through the hole in the wooden top daddy made. The churn held about five gallons, but we only filled it about two-thirds full. Mama considered that to be the best amount for churning. The way we churned butter was by sitting in a chair next to the churn and vigorously bringing the dasher up and down. This churning further separated the cream, and butter formed. The butter floated to the top when made. After thirty or so minutes of churning and after removing the butter, we had a churn half full of really great buttermilk. It was very tasty and we drank a lot of buttermilk. Daddy crumbled cornbread into his and ate it with a spoon. I did not.

I usually met Wilse down by the barn on Friday mornings. We sat on the rocks he had placed there for that purpose and talked. Wilse waited on his rock until I arrived. He was not a big man, but impressive. His face, weather-beaten to the color and texture of dark leather, always broke into a smile when I arrived. It looked as if it might crack. His nose was large and hooked, with a pair of dark-rimed glassed perched on top. Bushy eyebrows overhung the glasses, and gray unruly hair protruded from beneath the worn, brown felt hat he always wore. His mouth turned down at the corners, perhaps as a result of years of having a heavy pipe hanging from one side or the other. He did not have a beard, but he nearly always needed a shave, and Friday was no different. That day he needed a shave rather more than usual.

There was one thing about Wilse I didn't understand. That was his high-back overalls. Surely I am not the only person who ever got poop on the high back when doing a Number 2. It was hard to get all that extraneous material out of the way. I only had to do that once to become an enemy of high-back overalls. Wilse had a pair of them on, nonetheless, and I saw a can of Prince Albert smoking tobacco poking out the top of the bib pocket. He wore an old gray work shirt and his Wolverine shoes with gray socks and a red band around the top. He was, as usual, glad to see me when I ambled up and took my seat on the other rock. I was wearing my Duck Head overalls with galluses that hooked at the bib and buttoned in the back. My shirt was white and my boots were Buster Brown.

Wilse held his pipe in his right hand and a match in his left as he tried to light the big S-shaped pipe. He winked at me and puffed on the pipe to stoke the fire before saying hello. I waited also and then responded. He sucked mightily on the pipe until smoke came out both nostrils and his mouth. Wilse sat with me and we waited. Mostly we talked. Wilse talked to me as if I were an adult equal to him. That day we waited for the mailman.

I think he expected Tom's check. Tom, his son, received a check from some-body because of getting shot in World War I.

"I b-b-been listening to t-t-that shortwave radio and them d-d-damn Germans are trying to f-f-fight again. B-B-Bastards will git us in another war before you k-k-know it." Wilse stuttered a little. "Tom says he ain't going b-b-back this t-t-time. They shot his ass once b-b-but he ain't giving 'em another crack at him. They shot yore Uncle Alton, too. T-t-t-that's why he limps so badly." Wilse sucked on his pipe, making popping sounds. Mama did not want me to spend so much time with Wilse because he cursed a lot. I knew not to say some of the words Wilse used. He didn't curse nearly so much as Albert Mofield, and Albert was only nine years old.

"T-t-they shot about an inch of b-b-bone out of Alton's l-l-leg in the battle of someplace. The d-d-doctors just jammed it together and tied it up and l-l-et it grow back, less about an inch. Alton s-s-says it hurts all the t-t-time and the only relief he gets is when he drinks a little whiskey. I th-th-think he drinks a lot of whis-whis-whiskey."

Uncle Alton got a check from the same place as Tom. Uncle Alton was mama's brother and he looked a lot more Indian than she did. One of their grandfathers was an Indian of some sort. Uncle Alton was dark-skinned with a round face and high cheekbones. He looked just like the pictures I saw of Tonto. He came to live with us from time to time. After a few months daddy would run him off , but always allowed him back if he promised to stay sober and leave the neighbors' wives and girls alone. Uncle Alton was what they called a ladies' man. There were several grown daughters around who became attracted to Uncle Alton. He beat the day-lights out of some guy at Sampson's Mineral Well when the man objected to Uncle Alton being overly attentive to some girl. Daddy sent him away after that.

"You mark my words, James Winfree, th-th-those d-d-damn Germans will start another war, and Roosevelt knows it and he will get us into the damn mess when it sh-sh-should only be Europe involved.

Tom won't ha-ha-have to go back but they will get my other boy, Crutchfield. You will be too young for it when it starts, but you may grow into it b-b-before it's over. Going to be a long war once it starts."

I sat and listened to Wilse update me on the German threat for at least two hours and came away as knowledgeable as anyone in a four or five mile radius. Wilse did not think much of the Germans, due mainly to their shooting both Tom and Uncle Alton. The rock became hard and I squirmed, but the conversation with this kind old man made me feel worth a thousand dollars. A thousand dollars was a lot to me in 1938.

Wilse was of the opinion the damn French were, "totally useless and don't have enough guts to defend themselves". Tom said, according to Wilse, he had rather have a German enemy than a French friend. Tom stomped around France fighting the Germans while the French spent their time hiding and surrendering at the first sign of trouble. Wilse said Tom got so mad that he personally shot three Frenchmen. Wilse kept up with the world on his shortwave radio.

Usually we talked about farming or how to pack a good load of tobacco in a pipe so it burned slowly and evenly. Smoking a pipe is an art. Many years later I bought five fine briar pipes and two or three cheap ones, and took up pipe smoking. I had tampers, scrapers, special lighters, pouches, pipe stands, and other items too numerous to list. Wilse just had one pipe and a can of Prince Albert. I often wished I had paid more attention to Wilse when he explained pipe smoking. After about a year, I decided smoking a pipe properly required an assistant. I had no assistant, so I quit. I gave the pipes to your daddy who, after deciding the same thing about pipe smoking, threw them away.

Sometimes we talked about women. Wilse knew a lot about women and was willing to tell me his secrets to better prepare me to deal with them when the time came. He did not prepare me well enough, I found out later. I have had a lot of trouble with women, especially with the one I married, your grandmother. But, as I said, whatever the subject, Wilse talked to me like I was a man, and when I talked to him he listened as he would to my father. I appreciated that.

*   *   *   *

Bad Gums, Good Whiskey, Hard Math

Wilse had trouble with his gums and the best treatment to ease the pain was to soak them in homemade whiskey. Since he could not remove his gums and soak them in a pan, he had to hold the whiskey in his mouth to get the full effect. He told me about one bad bout with painful gums. "Tom," he said, "walked to Rome to get some whiskey from the b-b-bootlegger. He lived on the road r-r-right in the fork, where the old road that went through R-R-Rome split off from the new road that bypassed R-R-Rome. The old man made the wh-wh-whiskey in a room of his house. He had a real wh-wh-whiskey-making still and all the extras he needed, including Mason j-j-jars and j-j-jugs."

Tom, it seemed to me, was very good about fetching medicine for his father. Even though I was still less than seven years old, I suspected Tom's interest lay more in the medicine than in Wilse's gums. Wilse kept the whiskey he used for his gums in the spring house just below the house where he lived. Wilse had a very good spring near by, almost as good as our spring and closer to his house. We had to walk about a quarter of a mile to get fresh spring water.

Mama handed me a small basket woven out of willow bark and said, "If you are going to meet Wilse this morning, take the basket and get the eggs at the hen house. The peddler comes today, and since you are going to be waiting anyway, you might as well get us some candy. Sell him whatever eggs you collect and buy candy with them. Get whatever you prefer. I am so hungry for candy I will eat anything."

The hen house, located about fifty yards from our house, was a pole-framed building with rough-sawed planks for siding. The planks were ten to twelve inches wide and one inch thick, lined up vertically as close together as possible, and nailed at the top, bottom, and middle to the pole frame. The hen house had a new roof made out of 1933 private passenger auto license plates.

There was one door to the building, on the left side of the front. It had neither lock nor knob. There was a big iron hook fastened to a link of chain bolted to the door. On the wall beside the door was a U-shaped hasp for the hook to go into when the door was closed. Inside the building three long poles ran diagonally from the ground, about three feet inside the building, to the roof at the opposite end. To build a roost for the chickens, we attached one of the poles to the inside of either side wall. The third we placed in the center of those two. We nailed small poles across the three slanted poles every two feet all the way from two feet off the ground to within two feet of the roof. The chickens roosted on these. We built a row of nesting places on the walls. The rows were twelve feet long, two feet wide and two feet high, divided into two-foot sections for the nests. This gave us six nests on each side of the hen house. The nests were about five feet off the ground, high enough to keep some varmint out and low enough for daddy and mama to gather the eggs easily. The roof for the nests was also made out of auto license plates.

It was hard for me to get the eggs from the nests, since I was not yet five feet tall. It was no thrill for me to reach into a nest above my head and out of my field of vision. Sometimes there would be a hen in the nest that did not want to give up possession of her egg. Also, egg-sucking black snakes sometimes got into the nests and, though they were harmless, a cold, coiled snake was startling when reaching for an egg. I was able to collect thirteen eggs.

Wilse and I talked about the continuing mess in Europe and damned the Germans and the French. Things were churning and stewing in Europe. He said Hitler blamed all of Germany's troubles on the Jews. He did not understand that. Of course, we had no experience with Jews. The only one we knew was Jesus, and though Wilse thought He had been a troublemaker at one time, we had no evidence He had any grudge against the Germans. He was, Wilse thought, mostly upset with priests, preachers, Romans, Gentiles, and other Jews.

Uncle Charlie had somehow acquired a radio with a shortwave band. I know he did not buy it. Uncle Charlie hardly ever spent any money. One night every week I would visit Uncle Charlie and we would sit up until early morning and listen to Hitler rant and rave. We had no idea of what he was saying but we could tell something was upsetting him. No one on the creek spoke any German.

Wilse and I heard the horn of the peddling truck in the distance. The peddler was probably at Mart Mofield's place. He usually blew his horn there to give Bill Mofield and J. R. Mofield notice he was on the way. Bill and J.R. lived on the old road, as did Hamp. There was no point in blowing for Hamp. He never went to meet the peddler. Actually, it was Bill's wife and Mrs. Lillie May that went to the peddling wagon.

About half an hour after we heard the horn blowing, the peddler rounded the curve just after passing the Kinslow place. It was a huge truck, Ford, I think, white with a faded blue stripe around the cab. The back was a huge wooden box that at one time was white. Faded red letters painted in large block style on the sides of the big box on the back of the truck advised everyone that this was a rolling store from Punch, Tennessee. There was a grocery in Punch and it owned the rolling store. It also sold gasoline at the store. It had a big sign of a flying red horse advertising its gasoline, Mobil, I believe.

The truck only had one seat. Where the second seat would have been was a walkway into the back of the peddling wagon to give the driver easy access to the bed. After stopping the truck in front of Wilse and me, the driver disappeared into the back and opened a large window that lowered to make a two-foot-wide shelf running the length of the big box bed. Inside were shelves full of canned goods and sacks and boxes of food and household items. There was a big case with drawers for storing eggs. The drawers had depressions covered with a soft material to protect the eggs from breaking while the truck bounced and banged over rough roads. A big scale, hung from an arm connected to the ceiling, would swing out so customers could see the weights of either sales or purchases.

The peddler was a big man, but not fat. We did not know any fat people in 1938. He seemed almost too big for the job, often bumping his head on pots or pans hanging from hooks screwed into the ceiling. He always had a big hello and smile for the women customers and most men customers. He had nothing for Wilse and only a weak smile for me. Wilse he knew had no money, and he suspected me to be equally broke. I did not let him put me off by his unfriendly attitude, and walked boldly up and handed him my basket of eggs.

"I want to sell you these eggs and buy some candy." He glared at me for a minute before asking if my mother knew I was there with the eggs. I pointed out her encouragement in the candy purchase.

He took my basket and said, "Eggs are twelve cents per dozen. How many do you have?" I did not say anything for he was counting them one by one and announcing the count in a loud voice. When he said "thirteen," he handed me the basket. He stood there for a minute mumbling, then took out a tablet and began scribbling on it.

"Eggs at twelve cents a dozen and you have thirteen. That means I owe you for one dozen and one egg. That comes to, uh, uh, or is it uh, uh." I glanced over at Wilse and he was grinning. The peddler mumbled and scribbled and uh, uhed several more times. Finally he put the tablet down, opened the cash drawer and removed a dime and two pennies before reaching into the egg drawer and removing one egg. Turning to face me, he said, as he handed me the twelve cents and one egg, "Eggs are twelve cents a dozen but I don't believe there is a man alive who can figure out how much I owe you for thirteen eggs. Take this'n back home with you. Now what kind of candy do you want?"

I started to tell him how much he owed me for the other egg, but Wilse said with a smile, "Get your c-c-candy and take that e-e-egg home to yore mama." I did.

I passed Uncle Sam on the way home. "I grabs, it's hot," he said. I didn't say anything, but on that February 11, 1938, it was 74 degrees. Uncle Sam was always saying, "I grabs." He usually knew what he was talking about when he said that. I guess 74 was indeed hot for February.

*   *   *   *

Chapter 7

Joe Kinslow's uncle was a holy roller preacher. I believe his name was Allen. He planned to have a revival service on the creek. I looked forward to the first night, but there was a lot of work first. The Rev. Kinslow wanted to build a brush arbor big enough to seat fifty people. A brush arbor is an outdoor shady place for meetings, picnics, or similar things. The way to build a brush arbor for a meeting is to go into the woods and cut a bunch of tall, slender saplings, some with a fork at the top, if possible. We cut the trees, trimmed the limbs off, and dragged the logs out of the woods to the brush arbor site with mules. We used J.R.'s wagon to haul the limbs and thick bushes out of the woods because we needed limbs with leaves, and also bushes to put on top of the arbor to make the shade. We used our mules and Uncle Charlie's mules to snake the logs because we had really high quality mules, better than anybody's on the creek.

Once we got all the logs and limbs out of the woods and over to the place where we were going to build the brush arbor, we went to work building it. Some of the men did not go into the woods but stayed at the building site and dug three rows of holes about ten or twelve feet apart with post hole diggers. Each row had four holes, each hole two feet deep.

Using our crosscut saw, we cut the bottom off the logs twelve feet below the fork. We cut twelve logs, one for each of the twelve holes to support the top that makes the shade. Once we got the posts in the holes and the forks pointed in the right direction, we filled the holes around the posts with the dirt that came out of the holes and tamped it in good to make each post steady and strong.

Once we completed the posts, we laid the other logs across the top of the posts in the forks to make the roof. We didn't have enough posts with forks, so we chopped a flat spot on one end of the pole going on top and fastened it to the top of the posts without a fork with a big nail and baling wire. Actually we tied all the poles in place with the baling wire because the holy rollers sometimes got really worked up and tried to climb the walls. We climbed up on top of the arbor and covered it with some old fence wire to support the bushes and limbs that would cover the top of the arbor. We used fencing staples to fasten the fencing to the log rafters. With that properly placed, the men covered the top with the bushes, limbs, and brush brought out of the woods on J.R.'s wagon. They were almost ready for the preacher to try it out.

Seats for the people who came to the revival meetings moved up to the top of the list on things to complete. The Rev. Kinslow had twelve or fourteen chairs, so we built benches out of old planks and the sawed-off ends of the posts to make seats for another thirty or so people. We worked on this for two days before the brush arbor was ready.

My daddy and mama were not holy rollers. They were Baptists, but not the foot-washing kind. They were Missionary Baptists. Many of the men helping were not holy rollers either, but it was just neighborly to help. Also, it was great fun to attend the meetings. I could hardly wait. I just loved the tambourines, fiddles, banjos, and guitars.

Going from our house toward Rock City, just a little way from our barn, the road forked. The left part of the fork followed the creek down past Hamp Mofield's house, J.R.'s house, Bill Mofield's house, and on to where Mart Mofield and Turner Mofield lived. Hershel Mofield lived there with his father, Mart Mofield. There, the left fork road crossed the creek and joined the main road that is really the right fork we built to get out of the creek. The fork started next to the Kinslow house, and there was a little triangle of land in the fork that was sort of community property. We built the brush arbor in that fork. Also, it was the spot where some of the traveling "tent preachers" pitched their tents and preached to the same group of people that listened to the Rev. Kinslow. The "tent preachers" were sort of boring. There was no shouting and no music like there was when the holy rollers got fired up with the message. Sometimes a bunch of knife swappers and peddlers set up a tent there and stayed a week or so, selling and swapping. They usually followed the Civilian Conservation Corps workers about and sold them whiskey and ginger beer, called "jake-leg." We called it jakeleg because bad ginger beer messed up your system, making it all jerky, especially your leg, which was apt to jerk and shake when you tried to walk. It soon became against the law to make, sell, or consume ginger beer. Mama outlawed ginger in any form for us, including in gingerbread. She also prohibited root beer.

*   *   *   *

A Molasses Break

The fork of the road was a busy place. In addition to all the preaching, it was the site of an annual community molasses-making. Two sides of the triangle were roads, and on the other side there was a big gully that ran water to the creek when it rained. The spot of land was not big enough for farming or any building, so it became community property used for most anything of value or interest to the people of Rawls Creek. Each year early in the fall, we set up on that small plot the equipment for making molasses. All the farmers brought their sorghum and squeezed the juice out of it and then cooked it off in big pans until it became molasses.

All the sorghum (we called it cane) brought there was clean and all the leaves, really blades, were removed before running it through the mill to squeeze out the juice. The mill was powered by a mule hitched to a harness and attached to a pole that turned the mill. The mule walked in a circle, turning the three big cylinders that squeeze out the juice. The pole was set up so it was about six feet above the ground, making it high enough for the workers to take a big bunch of cane and shove it between the rollers after the mule passed and before he got back. Three rollers made three places to shove in the cane, and that meant the workers fed the cane from three different stands with a man stationed at each stand. Cane went in one side and had to come out the other side, and when it fell to the ground it quickly piled up and blocked the workers who fed the mill. Therefore, another team of three men took the squeezed cane away. Also, there was a tub to hold the juice and a replacement tub. That took another two men because the tub of juice was heavy. They moved the juice over to the cooking pans. The mill required a team of eight men and a mule to keep it moving at full steam. We had to do our jobs in a responsible and timely manner to get the most production out of our work.

Making molasses required three cooking cycles. The first pan cooked the fresh juice until it foamed. Then it was moved to the second pan in which it cooked until the foam subsided. Last came the third pan In which it cooked until it became the proper consistency of molasses. When it was finished, we drained it off into jars, cans, or glass jugs.

Each farmer knew how much cane he had brought and how much juice came from that cane. There was more juice than molasses because some of it cooked away, but we knew how much molasses came from five gallons of juice. All our friends were honest, so everyone got the proper amount of molasses even if he was not there to help with the making..

*   *   *   *

Break is Over

Now back to the holy rollers, so called because when the spirit got them and wouldn't let them go, they reacted by rolling on the ground, or floor if inside. Sometimes the spirit made them get happy and they shouted for joy or spoke in unknown tongues. That is, they were saying words or making sounds no one understood. Joe Kinslow and I thought that was silly.

No one cared a whit about what Joe and I thought. My parents and grandparents came from the old school that believed children were for seeing, not hearing. They also believed the men ate first, the women ate second, and the children ate last, and if we missed out on the sweet potatoes or squash, that was too bad. Mama always saved me a piece of her chocolate pie or the gingerbread without the ginger. I had just as soon missed the gingerbread. It just wasn't the same without ginger, but I did not want to get jakeleg. Joe Kinslow liked the gingerless gingerbread. Joe liked everything. I know now that was because he did not get much of anything at home except grits and mush.

*   *   *   *

I am sure you have never heard of mush. Your father told me you had never had a bologna sandwich. That being true, I am certain mush seldom appears on your menu. I personally think bologna in better for you than those chicken nuggets from McDonalds. They have no taste other than salt and grease, and I suspect, mighty little chicken.

*   *   *   *

The Rev. Kinslow put up posters on posts and trees announcing the beginning of the revival on Tuesday, August 17, 1939, at 7:00 p.m. We finished the brush arbor on Sunday but the Rev. Kinslow insisted on starting on Tuesday rather than Sunday night. He had a reason for this that made no sense to me, but did to everyone else. Tuesday fell on the first quarter of the new moon and, according to the Rev. Kinslow, the first quarter of the moon was the best time to start a revival. It was true that we planted seeds and bred horses and cows according to phases of the moon. But why would the moon affect a revival? I did not know. I still don't.

By Monday afternoon I knew waiting for the moon was going to be a mistake. Any fool could tell by the signs in the air and sky that rain was on the way. Daddy and I planned to go the first night of the revival, but we got a little nervous about the weather. Mama would not go with us. She put holy rollers in the class with Dr. Sloan. She didn't have any truck with holy rollers. August is usually hot and dry, but the signs for Tuesday were ominous. My goodness it was hot! The sky became dark and full of clouds on Monday. I was only six years old but I knew if it was dark, cloudy, and windy on one day, it was more than likely to rain the next. I didn't care what phase of the moon was operative. Rain, like tomorrow, rolls in. The Rev. Kinslow put his trust in the moon. He should have been watching the sky and feeling the air.

Sometime Monday night, or maybe Tuesday morning, the rain beating on the roof awoke me. I had no clock or watch, so I didn't know the time. I had my own room in the loft. There was a stairway beside the chimney in the big bedroom of the house where we lived then. We had moved up to the house on the hill after daddy and Uncle Charlie put a new roof on it with the auto plates, the brown and cream ones. It made a pretty roof and did not leak.

The heavy rain beating on the metal roof made a loud noise. There was one little window at the end of the room and the rain beat against it with determination. My room lay under the roof, shaped like a triangle. I could stand up in the middle of the room from end to end but the sides went down to the floor, and the standing up area for me consisted of a strip about twelve feet long and four feet wide. The entire room was about nine feet wide, but the ceiling, really the roof, went to the floor.

Looking out the window, I could see nothing. It was nighttime and raining harder than I had ever seen before. I thought about the problem the rain was going to be for Brother Kinslow. A brush arbor will keep off a little rain, but not a rain like that. Even if the rain stopped by noon, the bushes and brush, full of rainwater, would be dripping on anyone under the arbor. I no longer expected to be among those present for the first night of preaching. Daddy was loath to get wet at a brush arbor meeting. Back to bed was my best option, and that is what I did. After a while the rain drumming on the metal roof seemed to develop a sort of steady rhythm, a rhythm that made sleep not only possible but also desirable.

Mama banging around in the kitchen awoke me early in the morning, and I quickly made my way downstairs to check on breakfast. With all that rain falling, mama didn't go to the smokehouse to get a new sack of sausage, so we made do with whatever she had in the house. That was Quaker Oats cooked. With butter and sugar, that was hard to beat for breakfast. I liked Quaker Oats.

It was hot in the kitchen, and damp as well. It was all that rain and the wind. It was very unusual to have such a hard wind with rain as heavy as it was that Tuesday. The wind blew the rain into the open windows and spread the dampness all through the large house. Rainwater streamed across the front and back porches while dampness pervaded the four rooms downstairs and crept up to the two rooms upstairs. One of the rooms upstairs was unfinished and used for a junk room. Aunt Florence called hers a "plunder" room. Her plunder looked like our junk. The space downstairs consisted of two bedrooms with a chimney between and a fireplace on either side. Each bedroom opened onto the front porch and entry into each bedroom was available through a door between the rooms. The front porch was four feet off the ground with wooden steps in the center, leading down onto the front yard. Daddy put a low wire stock fence around the porch and a gate at the steps to keep Geraldine from falling off. I considered myself too smart to fall off the porch.

The other two rooms were the kitchen and the dining room. Access to those rooms from the bedroom on the right was through a door into the kitchen, and a door in the other bedroom led into the dining room. A framed opening between the kitchen and dining room allowed free flow of traffic between those rooms. Builders considered hallways wasted space in those days. It was a bigger and nicer house than the house down by the creek, where mammy and pappy lived. On the outside it had unpainted weather boarding. On the inside the walls had paper with pretty printed patterns, except for the kitchen. There was something called felt on the kitchen walls, a dark gray material. Daddy threatened to paint or paper over it, but hadn't as of that Tuesday.

*   *   *   *

I learned to cook early

Our kitchen stove, manufactured of cast iron by Magic Chef, was black. It had six heater plates, a big oven underneath, and three warming ovens above, two with doors and one without. Daddy kept a big pile of stove wood on the back porch next to the kitchen door. The firebox, where the wood burned, was on one side. At the back of the stove and on the other end, there was the flue with a long black stovepipe going up through the roof. The suction from the stovepipe pulled the heat in the firebox under the heater plates and around the oven, then up the flue. That was the way heat transferred to all the cooking surfaces of the stove. Knowing how to load the firebox properly was the key to controlling the temperature of the oven and the cooking surfaces.

I knew how to do it and I knew how to cook. A few days previously I had come home from school and found a note saying, "Gone to Rock City." I had time on my hands, so I made a cake. The first thing I did was get the ingredients together. First was flour. I had plenty of that. Second were eggs. Two or three was what mama used. I knew there were plenty of eggs in the hen house, so I set off to get them. Hens occupied the nests and that was strange for late in the day. Usually the hens flocked by the corncrib, waiting to be fed. I gave two or three hens a healthy poke with a stick and they left the nest. I selected three large eggs for the cake.

The next ingredient was sugar. Once again there was plenty of sugar in the kitchen, but no milk. The recipe called for one or more cups of milk, as needed. While I was on the way to the hen house I noticed Stella Dallas and Our Gal Sunday, two of our Jersey cows, out by the barn. It was easy to get two cups from Stella Dallas. Now all I needed was some vanilla flavoring. I knew there was plenty in the kitchen because the Watkins Man had come by the previous week. Mama never ran out of vanilla flavoring.

I fired up the stove, mixed my cake ingredients, and put the mixture into a round cake pan that I had greased with butter. The thermometer on the stove moved slowly up to 350 degrees. When it reached the desired temperature, I slid the pan into the oven and cooked it on the center rack until brown on top and thoroughly finished. While placing the cake in the oven, I had noticed mama had left two smoothing irons on the stove. Probably she had ironed our clothes. I really liked starched and ironed clothes as my mother did them. Hardly anyone in school had starched and ironed clothes. It was not easy for mama to do it, having to heat the iron and all, but she did it.

I went to my *Fanny Farmer's Cookbook* while the cake baked, and looked at the recipe for icing. It instructed me to sprinkle the cake with about a quarter of a cup of confectioner's sugar. To me sugar was sugar and all we had was a hundred pound bag of it, so I sprinkled the cake liberally with the granulated sugar. It made a beautiful cake.

Late in the afternoon on the day the revival was to start the rain was still pouring down in buckets full at a time. Daddy looked at me and he knew from my expression that I knew what he was going to say; therefore he said nothing. I knew we were not going to the brush arbor revival that night. Daddy preferred dry over wet.

Thursday morning the sun came out bright and hot and quickly dried up the moisture left over from the rain. Out on the front porch, looking north, I noticed the clouds breaking up and big patches of blue sky showing through the breaks. Old Pete and Jug looked very happy that morning. They, like my father, preferred dry over wet. Old Pete was getting pretty old and a bit short tempered with Jug, who was just a pup. Pete was solid white except where stained by dirt or berries or something, and no particular breed of dog dominated his appearance. Jug in contrast was some sort of terrier and something else, but mostly terrier. He had chin whiskers. I supposed he had a chin under those whiskers. Pappy and Uncle Sam did. Old Pete and Jug were my friends and stayed with me as much as possible. Old Pete understood more about boys than Jug. Joe Kinslow and I liked to "rassle." Jug always thought Joe was hurting me and had bitten him three or four times. Later Joe became reluctant to wrestle with me.

Jug seemed to have a kidney problem and quite often peed on the persimmon tree in the front yard just to the left of the lilac bush. The persimmons were just about ripe then and I hoped mama would make a persimmon cobbler. She seldom objected to making the cobbler, but did not like to seed a gallon of persimmons. Sometimes she left the seeds in and let us take them out as we ate. This was OK unless you forgot about the seeds. Small and hard like marbles, they were not round but oval-shaped. Mama did not approve of Jug peeing on the persimmon tree and told daddy to do something about it. But he hadn't. More than once she threatened to "Cut that dog's pisser off." Joe and I also peed on trees, but we carefully avoided the persimmon tree.

The persimmon is sort of similar to a plum but is not one. The fruit is either yellow or orange-red when ripe. Ours was the orange-red type and very tasty when ripe, but very bitter when green. Daddy said the tree's name came from the Cree Indians' name for the tree, meaning "dried fruit." Daddy said the real name was pasiminan and that the early settlers could not pronounce it properly and called it persimmon. Daddy was smart like that. It has been probably thirty years since I have seen the old house. I think I will go back soon and see if the persimmon tree is still there. It is the only one I know of anymore. Of course, I have not made a study of persimmon trees.

There was a big rose of Sharon bush by the left corner of the porch, with a profusion of purple flowers. It was really pretty. On the other corner a climbing rose bush climbed all over the corner and up to the roof, scattering a mass of red roses. Daddy told us the rose of Sharon is native to the Sharon area of Israel, and mentioned in the Bible. As I said, daddy was smart like that. The holyhock is part of the same family of plants, and we had several that grew each year to about four or five feet and bloomed with big red flowers. We planted them in the drip of the roof and they did very well there.

As I said earlier, by Thursday everything was dry, and daddy and I were back on schedule for going to the preaching. Joe Kinslow and I hoped the spirit would grab the guitar picker and cause him to beat his guitar against the posts again that year. Clifton Mofield still marveled at the guitar picker's actions two years before. Clifton would be there Thursday night with Joe and me.

Daddy and I, in our clean and freshly starched and ironed overalls, picked out a seat near the front. Daddy would not sit on the front row and implored me to follow his admonition, "Never sit on the front row at church." His reason went back many years, when as a boy in the New Middleton Baptist Church, he fell asleep on the front row. It was during a particularly boring sermon and he rolled out of the pew onto the floor right at the preacher's feet. From that point forward, daddy wanted something in front of him to block a similar roll.

Looking at the crowd as we hunted a seat, I saw Mrs. Cowline (I think her name was Caroline, but we called her Mrs. Cowline) Marks sitting with her daughter, Lassie Lee. Wilse was in the back leaning against a post with Hamp Mofield. I did not see Tom or Crutchfield Marks, but I bet they were there somewhere. J.R. and Lillie May Mofield were sitting with Bill Mofield and his wife and daughter, Alma. Mart and Mrs. Matt Mofield turned up also. Turner Mofield leaned against his car, parked near the brush arbor. The Kinslow crowd, Thomas Kinslow and his family, occupied the entire front row. Uncle Charlie and Aunt Florence sat in the middle of the arbor with Horace Flippen, Fred Taylor, and Mary Alice. Thomas and Minnie Lester sat with their son, Howard, and their neighbor, Earl Underwood. Mrs. Mary Underwood and her mother, Melissa Highers, were not there. They belonged in the same group with my mama: no truck with holy rollers.

A.J. Mofield came with his wife and their two boys, Albert and Julian. Lee, John M., Trigger, and Fay Lee Mofield were there, but I did not see Lee's wife until I noticed her over on the side, talking with Lydie and Jesse Poston and Harry and Neva Jenkins. Red and Haskiel Jenkins stood well back and talked to Marcellus and Clifton Mofield. We called Clifton "Tit." I don't know why, but it stuck with him. May Poston and A.J. Allison walked up and spoke to daddy. A.J. was married to Mr. May's daughter. She and her mother stayed home. All the Napiers arrived late and both Marvin and Robert waved to me. We were friends. Miss Parelee came with them. I have no idea of her actual name, but we always called her Miss Parelee. Aunt Arther and Uncle Andy took seats with the Napiers, as did Aunt Babe and Uncle Sam Enoch. John Steelman and his son, Robert, cornered Uncle Sam, and John delivered one of his long harangues about something. I did not see Mrs. Steelman but I am sure she was there somewhere. She was the reverend's sister. Up near the front, a large group of people I did not know milled around, hunting places to sit. They usually followed the reverend around to all his meetings. I think they came from Punch and Plunket's Creek.

*   *   *   *

I have taken a lot of space here to recite all the names of the people present because I want to point out to you that I knew all those people and that they meant a lot to me. They were the people I grew up with during my first twelve years, and they helped form the better parts of my character. I do not blame any of them for my many flaws. I especially want to call your attention to Wilse Marks and the affect he had on my life. I also want to say how much I regret letting him and his sons die without ever acknowl-edging my love and respect for Wilson Marks, known to friend and foe alike as Wilse.

*   *   *   *

The Kinslow house was just across the road from the brush arbor, and five men and five women came running out of it carrying two guitars, two banjos, one fiddle, and four tambourines. The meeting was about to start. The Reverend Kinslow asked the crowd to clap their hands and we did. The group burst into about thirteen verses of "The Royal Telephone." None of us had a telephone, royal or otherwise, but we knew what it was. After that the other songs seemed tame and I do not remember the name of any of them.

Brother Wheeler, who came with the Rev. Kinslow, prayed for a long time after the singing. He thanked God for everything he could think of and asked God to bless all of us and make us pour out our hearts and souls to Him and our pockets to the Reverend Kinslow. Uncle Charlie, not one to empty his pockets foolishly, did not amen that portion of Wheeler's prayer. After the prayer, the Reverend Kinslow set in to preaching. At first he spoke low and slow, causing us to lean forward to hear. As he pro-gressed, he got louder and louder, and near the end he was speaking in unknown tongues. His message contained a lot of hallelujahs and amens, not to mention a load of "and uhs." Nevertheless, he hammered his mes-sage home, and three women and one man began to shout. They were the ones from Punch.

Our group appeared unmoved except for Aunt Florence and Lilie May. They were beginning to jerk and roll their heads. I noticed Uncle Charlie gave Aunt Florence a pretty hefty nudge with his elbow. The spirit moved on and Aunt Florence settled back into her regular slump. I looked at Joe Kinslow sitting across the aisle, and he looked back at me. Disappointment hit us hard. No one had banged a guitar or banjo against a post. We did not lose hope. There were three or four more days to go before this revival ended.

*   *   *   *

Chapter 8

Our main barn was located right on the road, just before the bridge we built over the creek to help the few cars and trucks that traveled our road. Before we built the bridge, the road went in front of our house, across the creek and up the far bank, and made a sharp left turn before going on its way. The bridge made travel easier for motor vehicles and did away with the sharp left turn.

There is a small sand bar in the creek just west of where horse and mule-drawn vehicles crossed the creek. Joe Kinslow and I played on the sandbar when the weather was warm and dry. The creek was maybe two feet deep and ten feet wide from the sandbar to the south bank. Water stayed in that pool almost all year. I have since learned that Joe and I were not nice boys. We enjoyed playing with the crawfish that lived in that pool. Most of the crawfish were about three inches long and easily irritated. Joe and I liked to irritate them. On either side of their heads was something resembling a tiny scoop. Joe and I learned the scoops, whatever they might be, had a lot to do with the crawfish's ability to crawl. Joe was not afraid of the crawfish. I had no fear of crawfish, but I found them sort of repulsive to handle and let Joe do that. Also, they would pinch your fingers and hurt. My hands were not as tough as Joe's and the pinching did not bother him.

Joe caught a big crawfish, maybe four inches long, and held him while I filled one of the scoops with sand. Joe put the crawfish down on the sand bar and we watched him. He couldn't crawl but rolled over and over, then flopped around until some of the sand fell out of the scoop. Then he could crawl again, but only in a circle in the direction of the scoop with the sand. After we watched him flip and flop for a while, Joe picked him up, washed him off in the water, and then placed him back on the sandbar. Once again the crawfish could crawl freely and moved off away from Joe and me. Sometimes we had eight or ten crawfish flopping and flipping on the sandbar.

Daddy's temper showed when he caught Joe and me messing with the crawfish. He explained that the scoops were the crawfish's ears and contained his sense of balance and equilibrium. When we put sand in his scoops, we messed all that up. He also said if Joe and I wanted to know what it was like to have our balance and equilibrium messed up, he would fill one of our ears with sand. We vigorously declined to experiment. The better part of valor, we determined, was to not mess with the crawfish until daddy went to Carthage for a meeting of the county court.

*   *   *   *

My Aunt Maude

It was early in June, shortly after one of our regular April floods, when Aunt Belle and Uncle Bedford promised to come get me for the visit we had discussed during Christmas. Aunt Belle was one of daddy's sisters. Another one was Aunt Maude. She was a free spirit before her time. She firmly believed a woman had an obligation to be a lady, or at least to act the part. A lady, she believed, always dressed her best and made herself up to look her best. With Aunt Maude this meant not only her best clothes and hats, but also a corsage, or at least a flower, at all times. To maintain her appearance and wardrobe required money, a scarce commodity for most.

This was no problem for Aunt Maude who, at the age of seventeen, married Mr. Baker, a wealthy widower and farmer in the town of New Middleton. Mr. Baker was, if my memory is correct, fifty years of age at the time of his marriage to Aunt Maude, and the father of six. During the ensuing years, he and Aunt Maude produced another six. Their life together was happy and successful. They remained married until his death.

Maude was a nature lover. She grew flowers and plants and always had a large and colorful garden. She was also an excellent cook, preparing elaborate meals, and often added rose petals to the plates to enhance the beauty of the food. Beauty, Aunt Maude believed, should be a part of any meal, regardless of how meager or bountiful. She was not a vegetarian but definitely a supporter of vegetables, usually having four or five with her dinners. I remember the first time she introduced me to fried pumpkin blossoms and dandelion greens. I was basically a pork eater, with potatoes, corn, and turnip greens. The meal she fed daddy and me once when we visited her during the middle of the week was a Sunday dinner by anyone's standards. She had pork roast, squash (it was the first time I ever saw squash), green beans, fried corn, boiled potatoes with parsley, and dandelion greens with fried pumpkin blossoms. After encouragement and cajoling from Aunt Maude, I tried the greens and pumpkin blossoms. They were delicious. Even daddy ate them with enjoyment. Curious, I asked Aunt Maude how to cook that stuff. I was a good cook and wanted to learn more. Here is what she told me.

"Put a little grease in an old black skillet and add some onions and garlic, and cook slowly for a spell. While that is cooking, tear the green off the dandelion greens and chop the stems. Toss the stems and greens in the skillet with the grease, garlic, and onion mixture. Cook until the greens wilt. Add salt and pepper and serve with crumbled fried bacon and a few pumpkin blossoms or rose petals that have been dipped in beaten eggs, then dusted with flour and fried."

I could handle all of that except the garlic. We had no garlic. Personally, I did not know there was something called garlic. Aunt Maude gave me a head of garlic that she grew in her garden. No one on Rawls Creek ate pumpkin blooms, roses, or garlic, as far as I was aware.

Aunt Maude and I were friends until she died. I never saw her without her flower or flowers, or when she was not looking her best. She came to visit me once when she must have been in her eighties. At that time her husband was Mr. Hatcher, her third or fourth, and also her last. Mr. Hatcher was a retired schoolteacher and retired postman. "Getting three pensions," Aunt Maude told me, "one from teaching, one from the Post Office, and his old age pension. Mighty sickly now, though. But I am not worried. I've got another one on ice if something happens to Mr. Hatcher."

The wife and I had just built a new house when Aunt Maude came by to see it and us. It was our dream house, later our nightmare house. The covering on the outside walls consisted of bleached and grayed western cedar planks. Inside, the ceilings in living and dining areas were sixteen feet to the center, sloping to ten on the side walls, and made of boards two by six inches by twelve feet on top of exposed beams. The ceiling and beams, as well as the paneled walls, were unstained at the time. Aunt Maude, impressed with our house, complimented us quite liberally, I thought. Later, I learned she told one of her many nieces that it was too bad about me. "The house is nice," she said. "It's just too bad James ran out of money before he got it finished. The outside needs painting badly, and on the inside the rafters are showing. It needs a ceiling." We were all sad when Aunt Maude died at about ninety. She did outlive Mr. Hatcher, but she never did get the next old boy off the ice.

*   *   *   *

Going to Rome, Rome, Tennessee, That Is

Aunt Belle and Uncle Bedford, true to their word, arrived on a Monday morning in their surrey, pulled by an ancient but lovable mare. The surrey did not have fringe on top but did have several small balls hanging around the top. They bounced and twisted as the surrey rolled along. It was called a surrey because it had two seats, bench type, for four or more people. A buggy was primarily a conveyance for two people having only one bench seat. It might have only two wheels. A surrey always had four wheels and a flat top. Both buggies and surreys usually were pulled by one horse. However, surreys occasionally were pulled by two horses, buggies never were. Uncle Bedford let me sit up front between Aunt Belle and him and drive.

The old mare had a good gait and could trot along for hours. If the road was rough Uncle Bedford let her walk, but when the road smoothed out, he clicked a couple times with his mouth and she broke into a trot. The surrey wheels would sing and crunch the gravel in the road as we sped along. We passed the Kinslow house on the right, and on the left, Hamp Mofield's place, J.R. Mofield's place, then Bill Mofield's, and on to Mart Mofield's until we came to Lee Mofield's house on the right. Jesse Poston's farm was just across the creek from Lee's. At the end of Poston's property, a road joined the Rawls Creek road. I don't believe it had a name. We took that road, crossed the creek, and passed Harry Jenkin's farm. Harry's house was on our right.

I was in new country after passing Harry Jenkin's house and did not know any of the people that lived further on toward Uncle Bedford's home. We climbed a steep hill. The road was rough and the old mare plodded along at a slow walk for what seemed a very long time. On the other side of the hill the road dropped down to the edge of the bluff along the high side of Round Lick Creek, and followed the bluff to Uncle Bedford's house. It sat on the left side of the road and backed up to the edge of the bluff, two hundred or three hundred feet above Round Lick

Creek. The road continued another three hundred yards, then intersected with U.S. Highway 70S about a hundred feet east of the bridge across Round Lick Creek. The bridge crossed the creek a few hundred yards south of where Round Lick Creek emptied into the Cumberland River, and only a tenth of a mile east of Rome. Ike Napier ran the ferry that crossed the river at Rome to the road to Riddleton and places north, quite unknown to me and quite forgotten today.

Lorena Capleanor, Aunt Belle and Uncle Bedford's daughter, married Louis Capleanor, a prominent farmer near the Rome community. Louis' brother lived on a big farm just across the river from Rome. Lorena and I visited there from time to time, getting Ike to take us across the river in a canoe. I really enjoyed those trips across the river, but I never talked too much about them to mama.

"You'll get drowned, you'll get drowned," she said. I never did. Neither did Lorena.

Aunt Belle had a nice house with modern furniture, a big kitchen, and a long front porch. It was a better house than ours. I enjoyed my visits with Uncle Bedford and Aunt Belle. She always had bread bought at the store in Rome: She called it light bread. I liked it with syrup better than with her biscuits. Uncle Bedford preferred the biscuits. Both were good. I got good biscuits at home but no light bread.

Uncle Bedford insisted his syrup be made a special way. Aunt Belle could not just pick up a bottle of syrup at the store and serve it to Uncle Bedford. Not on your life. The way to make the syrup to satisfy Uncle Bedford was simple. Aunt Belle would heat a pound of brown cane sugar in a heavy saucepan until it melted and began to bubble. To the saucepan she added a pint of Karo's dark syrup and mixed and stirred until it was hot. She then transferred the mixture to a can or syrup bowl. It was delicious with butter over light bread.

At Aunt Belle's I would stand in the back yard on the edge of the bluff and look out over the bottom land along Round Lick Creek and across the river. Rome, with its three stores, Dr. Fisher's place, three churches, and the twelve or fourteen houses, was a spectacular sight to me. It may have been unusual for a person of my age to stand on a bluff and just look at the view for thirty or more minutes, but for me it was normal. The view was beautiful: rows of corn in the bottoms, trees along the bluff, ferryboat on the river, and the busy main street of Rome. From time to time, there would be a car, two or three buggies, and a wagon in the middle of Rome.

I was reminded of a time not too long before when it rained so much and so long we expected to see Noah come floating by in his ark. After what seemed like months the rain stopped and the sky brightened. I wondered where the dark, ominous clouds went and how they went so quickly, making way for the sun. Daddy suggested he and I take a ride down to Aunt Belle's on the two old horses we had. We didn't have but one saddle, so I had to ride bareback with just a couple of grass sacks for cushioning. That was OK with me and with the mare.

We passed Uncle Sam on the way and he said, "I grabs, CS, it's wet." As usual, when he said, "I grabs," before his words, he was correct. This was before the day of the complete domination of the waters of the Tennessee Valley by the Tennessee Valley Authority, so flooding was commonplace. When we arrived at Aunt Belle's, there were several people in her back yard standing on the bluff looking at the water. All the bottom land along Round Lick Creek was under water, as was the bottom land across the Cumberland River. The framework of the bridge across Round Lick Creek poked through the floodwater that covered it as well as most of Rome. Ike Napier had the ferryboat tied up against the bluff next to his little store. It wasn't really a store, more of a bait shop: cane fishing poles, lead sinkers, hooks, line, floats, and worms and minnows; that sort of stuff. Uncle Bedford said, "Ike had better watch the river closely. When it starts to go down as opposed to rising, he is likely to end up with the ferry boat hanging off the bluff."

As Uncle Bedford spoke, I watched a rowboat enter the grocery store on the north side of Rome's main street. There seemed to be no danger of the river going down any time soon. The ferryboat was safe. James Gann's and Dr. Fisher's houses were up on the hill, safely out of the backwater on one of the other two streets in Rome. There were a few other houses up there, but I do not remember the owners. The Presbyterian Church sat on a small knoll just east of the grocery. The floodwater surrounded it on all sides, but it remained dry. The water never got in it, although it finally reached the steps. The Baptist Church and the Methodist Church occupied the high ground south of Rome, well away from the river or the backwater. I do not remember the year of that particular flood, but it was a regular occurrence until TVA dam-builders and lock-builders took total control of the water and stopped the regular flooding. People said the TVA stopped the temporary floods by creating permanent floods. The TVA called them lakes.

*   *   *   *

Danger Lurks Nearby

Across the highway from Uncle Bedford's house was, as I said before, Ike Napier's bait store, his house, and two or three other houses. Near the top of the hill was Pink Holliday's house. Pink (that was what everybody called him) had a son named Ray. He was about my age and we got along quite well. One day about noon I decided to walk over to Pink's house and let Ray know I was at Uncle Bedford's for a few days. It was a hot, dry, and dusty day near the middle of July. I wore my old straw hat to keep from frying my brain. Mama always said, "Put your hat on, James. That sun will fry your brain." It never did, but I always wore my hat. Pink had a nice house. However, the paint, or maybe the whitewash, had peeled off several years previously.

Mrs. Holliday said Ray had gone down toward Ike's store. I decided to see if I could find him. When I came to the third house (I knew the girl who lived there), I saw a man on the front porch talking to the people inside who were eating dinner. (You call it lunch, we called it dinner.) Perhaps they had seen Ray. If not, I could talk to the girl. I walked up onto the porch. The man on the porch, whom I did not know, was about daddy's age, but larger. He had on old corduroy pants, a dirty white shirt, and a flimsy straw hat. He needed a shave.

The house was not a fancy house by any standards. It was very rustic with barn siding and a rusty tin roof. The planks that made the porch were rotten and sort of chewed away at the ends by the drip from the roof. The roof had no gutters to channel the rain away, so it just ran off and splattered on the ground and the ends of the porch planks. Over time the ends rotted off. The front door seemed to open into the dining room, or perhaps the table was in the dogtrot between the kitchen and the rest of the house. I do not remember. But in any event, one step up from the porch would put you into the eating place. I was about to go in when I noticed there was a serious argument going on. A man seated at the table was yelling at the man on the porch, who was yelling back. I stopped on the edge of the porch and decided to wait until things quieted down.

There were three women of various ages at the table, along with the other man. The girl I wanted to see was not there. I noticed one of the women was old and wore a bonnet while eating. The man at the table said, "Get off my porch and out of my yard." I don't think the man on the porch heard him because he stepped up into the eating area.

"Don't drag yore ass into my house!" The man at the table got up and shouted directly to the other man who, unless he was deaf, could not avoid hearing. "I said don't drag yore ass in my house! Now git out of here!"

The other man did not obey. I'm sure he heard. I think the people in the grocery in Rome heard what the man said, so loudly did he say it. The man did not leave, but said something in a loud voice that I do not remember. I saw an old single barrel twelve gauge shotgun leaning against the wall behind the just-vacated chair of the man in the house. That man, wearing bib overalls with no shirt and a floppy felt hat, kicked the chair out of his way and picked up the shotgun, swung it around and stuck the barrel end against the intruder's Adam's apple. "I said get your ass out of my house!"

Apparently the other man did not move fast enough to placate him because he pulled the trigger. The gun made a loud noise and knocked the man flat of his back on the porch right beside me. I looked down and saw his head jammed in the hole between two planks with rotten ends and the porch support. Strange, but I remember his ears were sort of squashed up against his head. His eyes were open but were not looking at anything. There was a hole in his neck about the size of a broom handle, and smoke was coming out of it. I could see the dirt under the porch through the hole, but I didn't notice any blood. Suddenly I did not feel well and decided to go see Aunt Belle. I also thought it advisable to get my ass off the porch.

A short time later a considerable crowd had gathered at the house, causing Uncle Bedford to decide to walk over and see what was going on. I walked with him. The undertaker was leaving with the body when we arrived. Ray turned up and said that Dr. Fisher had pronounced the man dead, and had left in about two minutes. Ray reported that Dr. Fisher said a twelve gauge shotgun blast in the neck usually made breathing difficult, and people who are not breathing are dead. Dr. Fisher did not require a cutting open of the body to tell that the man was dead and what killed him.

Sheriff Gann was a friend of Uncle Bedford and walked over to say hello. "If a man with a shotgun tells you to get your ass out of his house, Bedford, you better go."

"What you going to do with him?"

"What can I do? He told him to get out. He should have gone. Not a problem for me or Baxter Key." Baxter Key was the district attorney. "He don't want to prosecute a man for something like this."

The sheriff was correct. We never heard of the incident again. He did ask me if I was all right. Someone had told him I was on the porch when it happened. I think it was the old woman wearing the bonnet.

Years later Lyndon Johnson described a level-headed East Texas voter in a way that put me in mind of that old woman, the shooter's mother, I think. Lyndon said, "A level-headed East Texas voter is one whose tobacco juice runs out of both corners of his mouth." That lady qualified to vote in East Texas. She dipped snuff, probably Brutons. She did not look the part of a Garrett user. That night Aunt Belle fixed me fried chicken and chocolate pie for supper, and made a big fixing of white gravy to eat over light bread. That was her version of "counseling," or maybe "closure," or whatever name the psychobabblers push today.

I never did find out why the dead man was on the porch or what the ruckus was about. But it sure is true that if a man with a shotgun tells you to leave you had better go.

*   *   *   *

The Yellow Airplane

It was in the summer of 1940 that Aunt Arther had her encounter with an airplane. I stood in the front yard between the two huge peonies growing on either side of the walkway, looking at the hollyhocks blooming vigorously in the shade of the porch roof. Suddenly I heard a loud roaring noise coming from the sky, and apparently so did Aunt Arther. She charged out of the kitchen door, the one beside the cistern, and out onto the porch, looking up into the sky. She turned the corner of the porch and headed toward the barn brandishing a dish towel in her left hand and a black skillet in her right, her print dress flying behind her. I watched her and forgot about the noise. Half way down the long side of the L-shaped porch, she spotted the yellow airplane, a double-winged job, as it passed over the barn at fairly low altitude.

Her speed increased and she yelled, "Andy, Andy!" As I watched goggle-eyed, she ran off the porch and made at least three steps in the air before she crashed to the ground in a heap. Gearldine, standing next to me, watched open-mouthed. When Aunt Arther left the porch, Gearldine began to squeal and laugh. She thought Aunt Arther was trying to fly. My dad, Uncle Andy, Wilse Marks, and Uncle Charlie missed the airplane while looking at Aunt Arther. They all began to laugh loudly. All, that is, but Uncle Andy, who dashed over to Aunt Arther to determine her injuries, if any. She rose to her feet rather unsteadily, adjusted her bonnet, and brushed off her dress. Seeing that she was uninjured, Uncle Andy began to laugh with the rest of the men. Aunt Arther, seeing nothing funny, swung at him with the skillet, adding to the laughter of the others as Uncle Andy fled into the barn.

*   *   *   *

The Frozen River

It was a cold northern wind that whipped the snow flakes painfully against any exposed skin. There was very little exposed skin in the crowd gathered on the south bank of the Cumberland River just below the bridge to Carthage. Daddy and I picked a place to stand on the high side of the road beside the rail spur. The coal unloading facility sheltered us somewhat from the wind. Daddy said we were all idiots watching idiots. It was cold, ten degrees below zero, as we saw on the huge thermometer mounted on the railroad building.

A T-Model Ford sat on the edge of the river along with the driver, a passenger, and a photographer from the Carthage *Courier*. It was a black (is there any other kind?) two-seater, with a canvas top and no side curtains.

There was a huge cedar log strapped on either side. If the ice broke, the logs would float the car, at least that was the theory. Daddy said they would make sure the car sank. Did I tell you the river had frozen solid several days before? The two people with the T-Model Ford planned to drive across the frozen river. I did not know why. There was a perfectly good bridge two hundred or three hundred feet up the river. Daddy allowed they were just naturally stupid folk.

The photographer unfolded his equipment as the passenger cranked the T-Model. It fired up easily and ran smoothly. Cautiously the driver moved the car onto the ice and headed across the river, encouraged by cheers and yells from the crowd. The T-Model picked up speed as it neared the center of the river, and seemed to leap to the other side, where an admiring crowd of people waited. The river crossing was successful. Encouraged, the driver spun the car around and headed back to our side. We thought him overly confident, but once again he was successful. The excitement over; the photographer was folding his equipment while hoping the driver did not try another trip. Daddy and I decided to crank up our own T-Model and go home via the road. I had a new brother at home. His name is Joe. He was born on the fifteenth day of the month before.

*   *   *   *

Chapter 9

Every man's religion

Religion was, I believe, more talked about than practiced on Rawls Creek. We had no church, which led me in the direction of talk rather than practice. The Highers and Underwood families were Campbellites and attended a church in Grant. They were regular churchgoers. Some Highers believed hell would be your home if you did not go to a Campbellite church on a regular basis. Mr. Earl Underwood was not of that strong an opinion. Quite often he stayed home. We were Missionary Baptists and believed in church going, but not as strict as Campbellites. More of the people on the creek were Baptists than any other brand, and went to the Flunketts Creek Baptist Church near Rock City.

Late one Saturday afternoon, a delegation of Baptists, tired of the trip to Rock City on Sunday, arrived to press their case for having church in the school. Daddy was not for it and had told them so several times before. That day they found him on the roof of our house taking a break from repairing a leak. This was the house near the creek and road. It did not have an auto tag roof.

There was a man and a women on the ladder talking with daddy. Three years previously he had married them. He could do that because he was a justice of the peace. Shortly thereafter, the couple decided to divorce and went their separate ways for a few months. Now they were back, asking him to remarry them. Daddy told them he properly married them the first time and had no intention of getting off the roof to do it again. "If you are serious this time, climb up the ladder and give me the license. I am going to charge you another fee. You did not get the divorce free. Put the money in the pocket of my jumper lying on the porch." He refused to say the words again, but signed the license. It was his opinion that their climbing the ladder was satisfactory acceptance of the wedding vows. This one stuck. They died in the 1980s, married for almost fifty years.

The leader of the delegation of Baptists waited patiently while the newly married couple descended the ladder and placed the fee in daddy's jumper pocket. They congratulated the remarried pair. Missionary Baptists were not much on divorce. Curing the divorce by remarriage was uncommon, but probably acceptable to them. We watched as the newlyweds, clutching each other's arm, climbed into the A-Model Ford parked near the barnyard gate. After a bit, the groom got out, inserted the crank into the appropriate aperture and gave it three healthy turns while the bride worked the spark. It roared into life, and after placing the crank in the boot, they roared off toward Rock City.

"Well, CS, are you going to talk to us from the roof?"

"If you are going to talk about church in the schoolhouse, I may crawl over the comb onto the other side. You know we will be criticized if we use the county's building for a church. There is always someone who will object to anything and everything. We will have no defense if a complaint is made. We will have to move. Obviously most of us can walk to the schoolhouse and that will make going to church easier, and that way maybe we can get a few more Mofields to come."

Daddy shinnied down the ladder and walked to the shade of the hackberry trees before continuing. "Last Sunday we went to church at Grant.

On the way back, just past the Hicks' house where the hill gets so steep, my old T-Model quit running. I cranked and re-tried the hill three times before I realized the gravity flow gas tank didn't have enough gas in it to cover the line to the carburetor when going up a steep hill. I finally turned the car around and backed up the hill so the gas puddled up in the end above the gas line. I do not like to do that anymore than you, but preaching in the schoolhouse is not the way to solve our problem."

Daddy did not know he was an advocate for separation of church and state. He just did not want problems with the school board. Daddy took one of the straight chairs under the trees, turned it around, back to the front, straddled the seat, and sat down in his best JP fashion, arms folded over the back of the chair. The church delegation sat in the remaining chairs, leaned against fence posts, or squatted in front of him. Some whittled, others chewed, smoked or spit as the spirit moved them.

For the next hour, conversation ranged from the need for a local church meeting place to the falling prices of tobacco, hogs, and corn. The discussion covered the rumor that Uncle Charlie was an active member of the kill-the-pigs group determined to deprive the money-grubbing sapsuckers in Chicago and New York of pork unless they paid a decent price to the farmer. Word was Uncle Charlie drowned twenty-three pigs in the creek, saying, "I am not going to feed my cheap-ass corn to these cheap-ass pigs to fatten some cheap-ass Yankee in Chicago or anywhere else. I am keeping enough for me and me alone." Daddy and I knew it was closer to a hundred pigs. Most of them we threw into Round Lick Creek just before it empties into the Cumberland River. No pork for the cheap-ass money-grubbers was our view. The hog farmers made this policy work, and by 1940, pork prices equaled beef. The drowned pigs had had a market value of nothing because nobody wanted them. In 1941, we sold hogs worth $25,000 and could have sold more if we had had them. Farmers never learn. Two years later there were more hogs than buyers and prices, while still better than during the drowning time, were only half those of 1941.

The conversation drifted back to the schoolhouse situation from time to time. Daddy finally agreed to discuss the proposal with the chairman of the school board, but he made no promise of recommendation.

*   *   *   *

Gone to Carthage

One morning daddy had on his light brown suit, tan shirt, and brown tie. His shoes were oxblood bluchers, old but highly polished. My daddy was five feet, eight inches tall with coal black hair and a thin, straight nose that was not aquiline and not Roman, but the best part of both. His eyes were dark brown, almost black, his mouth broad, full-lipped, with straight white teeth. My mother thought him a good-looking devil. So did most women. Mother was sending me to Carthage with daddy because she thought he was too handsome to be out alone. I was spotlessly clean and had on my best pants and shirt and newly polished white shoes. She wiped out the seats in the T-Model to prevent me from getting dirty before we got to Carthage.

Daddy parked the car in the reserved parking spaces in front of the courthouse. We set out to see the county judge, James Clinton Beasley, better known as Clint. He pronounced the wedding vows for daddy and mama on September 12, 1931, in his office in the courthouse. He charged no fee and I got the James part of his name. Lofton Fisher was the court clerk and he gave daddy the marriage license at no cost. I got the Lofton part of his name. I am often glad Bucking Richmond and Slicker Huffines did not have anything to do with the wedding.

Daddy's purpose was to discuss with Judge Beasley the propriety of allowing the Missionary Baptists to conduct church services in the schoolhouse. He worried that everyone else would want to do likewise, or that some other disturbance would result. The judge was a friend who gave him advice and counsel. I fidgeted for fifteen or twenty minutes before the judge concluded that church was an acceptable use of the facility. Afterwards, we ambled through the courthouse lobby speaking for brief periods with various visitors and officeholders, including Lofton Fisher. Lofton added his blessing to the Baptists' proposal and suggested daddy speak with the school board chairman.

By the time we got home, daddy had smiled at all the women in the courthouse, spoken to all the men, and reached an agreement with the school board. The agreement required the Baptists to keep the building clean and protect and not disturb school property, as well as student property. They also had to furnish coal or wood for the stove when needed, and fuel for the big gaslights. Access to the schoolhouse was from 10:00 a.m. to 12:30 p.m. on Sundays only. The Baptists, of which daddy was one, accepted this agreement. During the four years we attended church at the schoolhouse, no disturbance occurred except the "Great Shorts-Burning Episode." Even then, no one lodged a complaint, although the episode may have been the beginning of the end of church at the schoolhouse.

*   *   *   *

The Great Shorts Burning Fiasco

Other than the shorts fiasco, the most exciting event occurred in the summer of 1941 when we left Joe asleep on a bench beside the bookcase. We missed him just before we reached Fred Taylor's house. Daddy retrieved him without incident, except bickering with mama over who was to blame. Afterwards, Joe was loath to attend any type church service if it required him to leave the car.

The matter of the shorts-burning began when the Missionary Baptists acquired a new preacher. I don't remember his name. He was of the fire and brimstone ilk. He definitely believed that God is going to cast most of us into a lake of fire where we will burn for all eternity. Only by the most scrupulous adherence to the plan of salvation would we be able to avoid this fate. "Narrow (he pronounced it narr) is the path and straight is the way and few can follow it to salvation," the preacher would say. "God is a loving God, a just God, but a vengeful God if not obeyed, loved, and worshipped." He admonished us to remember God's treatment of the people of Sodom and Gomorra who were doing unspeakable things and violating God's laws. He pointed out how God was just and loving in the midst of the fire and brimstone he rained on the people and cities of Sodom and Gomorra. God allowed the just man, Lot, to escape with his family, but instructed them not to look back as they departed the doomed cities. Lot's wife glanced over her shoulder and, shazam, she became a block of salt. God does not have truck with people who disobey. Mama took after him.

I believe the preacher shocked the good people of Rawls Creek when he began to suggest many of them were guilty of sin. He intimated some of them were doing unspeakable things. Daddy's opinion was, "He has quit preaching and started meddling." Uncle Charlie snapped his coin purse closed and stayed home.

This change in the preacher, if it was a change, occurred gradually until it hit full stride in the spring of 1940. The men were grumbling and taking less interest in his sermons. The women, however, listened with rapt expressions on their faces and even shouted amen on occasion. The preacher said the men had lust in their hearts and minds. The women agreed. The men were, he said; "using women for satisfaction of their sinful animal-like lusts and purposes." This brought expressions of outrage from the men and the snapping closed of coin purses echoed from all quarters. At one point the preacher screeched at the top of his scratchy voice, "The men of this church are sinners and we need to help them and pray for them." This he did, pray that is, for a long time. The women joined in with amen.

Looking back, I find the preacher was wrong about the men. The Mofields all cursed, smoked, chewed, dipped, and probably some of them drank a nip now and again, but they were not sinners as portrayed by the preacher. The worse thing about the Hales was the horrible cake Mrs. Hale baked and forced on me from time to time, along with a cup of Mr. Hale's atrocious coffee. Uncle Alton smoked, chased women, and drank. He took regular nips for the pain he suffered because some German shot him in the leg. Uncle Alton told me many times, "Before I fell down I shot the dirty bastard right between the eyes." None of that was sufficient to make Uncle Alton a sinner, in my opinion.

Wilse and Tom Marks were honest, truthful, hard workers who drank, smoked, cursed, and chewed. Crutchfield was sort of a stick in the mud. But none of them were sinners of the preacher's description. Then there were Uncle Sam, Uncle Andy, May Poston, A.J. Allison, and Thomas Lester, all upstanding citizens who kept private their lives and certainly didn't commit any sins in public. Thomas may not have been all that upstanding, what with having to keep a weather eye on Minnie, his wife.

The Napier, Tuggle, Agee, and Preston men were beginning to be absent from church on a regular basis. I was of the opinion the preacher was losing his base of support. He liked a little money and the men had it all. And it seemed they were seriously thinking about keeping it in the bibs of their overalls.

By August of 1941, the preacher determined the cause of the men's lust and sin to be the women. "You are enticing them with your sensual behavior and scandalous dress. How can you expect men to respect you if you go around showing off your body to everyone? During the week I see kneecaps and even thighs. Some of your dresses, unbuttoned at the neck, expose more than they should. If you act like temptresses, how can you expect to be treated as ladies?"

This talk perked the men up to the point of all being present the next Sunday. Word got around quickly that the preacher "is taking off on the women." I studied over the preacher's words and tried to think of how many kneecaps and thighs I had seen in my years on Rawls Creek. Apart from the girls at school, it was not many. My list was short and I determined that the preacher must get around at a different time from me. My list included Lassie Lee, Minnie, Anna Lee, Mrs. Mary, and mama. Mama had taken to wearing shorts, as did several of the young, skinny women. The old women and the fat women avoided them like the plague. Mama's shorts were really short-legged pants, made by cutting off daddy's old pants at about the knee. I made a list of women who, as far as I knew, did not have legs. The list include Aunt Babe, Aunt Arther, Mrs. Cowline, Mrs. Highers, mammy, and many others. All wore long black dresses that dragged the ground, and black bonnets that covered their heads. For all I knew, they were bald. If their dresses had buttons, I never saw them.

Three weeks and three sermons of about an hour and a half each, full of references to Sodom and Gomorra, Lot's wife, and some lady who hung out at Virge Sampson's Mineral Well, led to overflow crowds. The old, the fat, and the ugly women exuberantly and excitedly supported the preacher. The young, the thin, and the pretty women demonstrated little excitement. Their husbands seemed to make up for their lack of support for the message. Daddy shook his head. Then came the lightning bolt.

"I am declaring Wednesday night to be a night of cleansing and for-giveness, as well as a time for rededication of your life to God," the preacher said. "Wednesday night we are going to meet on the corner by the Kinslow house and have a bonfire, a brief sermon, a prayer, and then the women are going to burn all the shorts and provocative clothing they own. Afterwards, we will hold a service of rededication." An almighty hush fell over the schoolhouse. Suddenly three old women began to shout and jerk like holy rollers. I did not recognize them. I think the preacher brought them along as shills. Albert Mofield was sitting next to me when the electricity in the air got the better of him. He darn near broke one of my ribs with his skinny, knobby elbow, and said, "Son of a bitch!" His mother, Belle, swatted him across the mouth. "God dammit, mama, that hurt." Belle swatted him again, harder.

"The Lord told me to look in that bookcase in the back of the room," shouted the preacher. "I did, and what did I find? Some of the devil's writing. There are sinful books in that bookcase the devil has put there to ruin the minds of these children. The Lord told me to have you good Christian people burn those books right on top of those evil shorts and dresses. Number one on the list is that devil's disciple, Mark Twain, that cigar-smoking, liquor-guzzling reprobate. And there are others in there that needs burning, too. Jesus don't want these pretty young children led down the path toward hell by these vile books. Get them out of there and we will burn them Wednesday night."

"Aw shit," said daddy.

Some of the women were expressing themselves by bellowing out loud amens and a few hallelujahs, as were several of the men. Aunt Florence began to jerk and the shills were shouting and foaming at the mouth. Someone, one of the Mofields I think, fainted. Several Kinslow holy rollers attended the service and they were at home in mass confusion, so they added to the furor by joining in the shouting. I elbowed Albert as viciously as he did me, and he said, "Son of a bitch." Belle was too busy with her dose of the spirit to notice Albert. A. J. lit his pipe and wished he had one of that damn Twain fellow's cigars. Geraldine began to squall her head off.

"Aw shit," daddy said.

The preacher was by now shouting amen and praise God at a fast pace. Right before my young eyes the Missionary Baptists were turning into holy rollers. Someone, or some two or three, knocked over Betty Underwood's desk and shoved Suedean's up against the stove. If I remember correctly, one of the shills did what seemed to be a version of the Charleston up on the stage, shoving the teacher's desk off the end of the stage when it began to interfere with her gyrations. Daddy said, "Aw shit" again. I figured he was happy the school board chairman lived up on Defeated Creek and was a Methodist. Mr. J.R. and Hamp Mofield came up to daddy and Hamp wondered if daddy wanted him to throw the preacher out the door. I wondered what Hamp was doing at church. I did not remember him ever being there before. Hamp liked to hunt, fish, and smoke on Sundays, maybe even take a nip of white lightning, thus committing the sins the preacher spoke of in his sermons.

This service was getting out of hand. It had to be stopped before more desks were overturned and the bookcase and books damaged or destroyed. Hamp and J.R. already had indicated daddy was the man in charge and daddy needed to act. He looked at mama, who rolled her eyes. Geraldine continued to scream. Shouters were beginning to swoon. Horace Flippen walked out the door. Suedean and Mary Alice followed him. Others of common sense were beginning to look troubled. Daddy charged up to the preacher. "Say a prayer and end this service and get those hauled-in shouters out of here," daddy said. "You burn one of this school's books and I will see you in jail. Now stop this. Now!"

The preacher noticed Hamp and J.R. moving up behind daddy and made a smart decision. He began to clap his hands. The three shills stopped shouting and gyrating, and the room quieted down. The prayer was short. The preacher was brave enough to invite everyone to the Wednesday night shorts-burning service.

On Monday morning, daddy and I set out early across the field beside our house, skirting Cub Nob, through the Highers' cornfield, and on to Mary Underwood's house. I did not want to go but mama insisted. She always made me go with daddy when she could. He was sort of long-legging it that morning and I had to run most of the time to keep up with him. We drank a cup of coffee with Mary and Earl before getting to the reason for the early morning meeting. Mr. Earl hunted me up a couple of teacakes to go with the coffee. Betty, their daughter who was about a year younger than me, was sleeping late, he told me as we searched for the teacakes.

Daddy and Mrs. Mary were in serious conversation in the dining room. Mrs. Mary was now our schoolteacher. Miss Gladys House had left for somewhere else and Mrs. Rogers did not work out. At daddy's suggestion, the school board hired Mrs. Mary, a good teacher. Early on in my life, even before she became the schoolteacher, she encouraged me to read. She had a connection with some outfit that sold old library books that were too worn to continue renting. She could buy these for a few pennies or a nickel each, sometimes a dime or quarter for real good ones like *Pilgrims Progress* or *The Grapes of Wrath* and *Magnificent Obsession*. My favorite authors were Zane Grey, E.B. Mann, Fran Striker, and Jack London. The books usually went for a nickel and Mrs. Mary sold them to me for the same price or let me borrow them, whichever I wanted or could afford.

She gave me several books by P. G. Wodehouse, Booth Tarkington and Francis Boyd Calhoun. Mama was particular about what books I read and sort of pitched a fit over a book entitled *My Lady Caprice*. Daddy said Mrs. Mary would not give me a book I did not need to read. Mama was not sure. After all, Mrs. Mary was a Campbellite, and a rather pretty one at that.

In *Penrod and Sam,* by Booth Tarkington, I found a paper apparently used as a bookmark, most likely before Mrs. Mary bought the book. Daddy and I looked it over carefully. It was a minister's license. given to G. C. Hessen by the Pentecostal Church of the Nazarene, Tennessee District Assembly, dated September 28, 1918, at Erin, Tennessee. The license was for one year. provided "his spirit and practice are such as becomes the Gospel of Christ, and his ministry corresponds with the established doctrines of the Holy Scriptures as held by the Church." Daddy did not think they "cut him much slack."

I bet daddy wished he had the Rev. Hessen at the Rawls Creek schoolhouse instead of the Missionary Baptists' shorts-burning, book-burning preacher he was trying to deal with that morning.

About the time Earl and I finished our coffee and teacakes, daddy ended his conversation with Mrs. Mary while they walked into the kitchen to freshen their coffee. There was a kind of smirk on Mrs. Mary's face. She enjoyed daddy's predicament rather more than she should, I thought. She told Mr. Earl that the Missionary Baptist preacher had turned out to be no more than she expected, just another holy roller.

She and daddy agreed to go to the schoolhouse and remove the books. The mood of the women and some of the men made it likely they would try to burn some of the books. How one preacher and three professional shouters riled the churchgoers into frenzy was more than Mrs. Mary could fathom. They decided to take the Underwood Plymouth and put the books in the boot. Rufus, the Republican, then living in Detroit, had left the car with Mrs. Mary and Earl. I think he left it because Milissa paid for it in the first place. Daddy had then moved up to the 1936 Chevrolet with "knee action," whatever that might be. We were not using his car because it had no boot.

We secured the few books the school owned in the boot of the Plymouth and Earl and Mrs. Mary gave us a ride down to where mammy lived. Mammy had a set of encyclopedia, 1896 vintage I think. She said she was going to burn the books on the shorts bonfire. Daddy said, "Bull shit, you are not burning anything." Aunt Babe and Uncle Sam heard the ruckus and came in. Daddy and I went home.

The great shorts-burning service occurred on Wednesday night, and although everyone in the community attended, it was a bit anticlimactic. There were no professional shouters and the spirit only made the crowd restless. After the singing, praying, and preaching, the women lined up, and one by one threw the sinful shorts and provocative dresses and blouses into the bonfire set up by the preacher. Aunt Florence had no shorts, so she borrowed a pair from mama, her last pair I think. Mammy threw the "S" volume of the encyclopedia into the fire while daddy was busy talking with Mrs. Mary. The preacher loudly began singing, "When the Saints Go Marching In." I thought that if I were in that number it would be without shorts. The fire blazed mightily and sparks flew as several other boys and I poked and stirred it with long sticks picked up near the creek. Daddy thumped me on the head when I appeared to be enjoying the service a bit too much.

After the final prayer daddy, who also was head deacon, took the preacher aside and told him it would not be necessary for him to preach on the next Sunday. The church would be trying out a new preacher, Brother Gladys Gregory. Missionary Baptists do that, you know. I never saw the preacher again. I never understood why Mr. and Mrs. Gregory name their son Gladys.

*   *   *   *

More Religious Problems

Early on a Monday morning, three months after the shorts-burning, Mary Underwood knocked on our door. She had driven the Plymouth almost all the way to our house. That was an amazing feat because the Chevrolet would barely make it over the rough road. We did not believe a Plymouth could possibly climb that rough and rocky hill. She talked animatedly with daddy and mama while I finished my breakfast. Then they all three hustled me out to the Plymouth to go to school. As Mrs. Mary, daddy, and I bounced down the rough steep hill to the main road in the Plymouth, they let me in on the reason for the early morning visit.

A group of holy rollers had broken into the schoolhouse and had a service of their own. They left a note expressing their view that the schoolhouse was as much theirs as the Baptists, and that they planned to continue having church there every Sunday afternoon. Just discussing the mess upset daddy, and since Mrs. Mary was with us, he said, "Aw shoot." He said it more than once.

He and Mr. Earl repaired the door and added reinforcing beams. Afterwards, he sent postcards to all the Baptists telling them he had closed the Rawls Creek church but that the Plunkett's Creek Baptist Church was still rolling along strongly. He threatened the holy rollers with jail. So ended four years of church in the Rawls Creek schoolhouse. I think daddy knew from the beginning that trouble always was just around the corner when turning the schoolhouse into a church.

*   *   *   *

War!

Daddy's relief at ending the religious problems at the schoolhouse did not last long. Actually, we attended only one or two services at Plunkett's Creek Baptist Church before his mind turned to other far more serious problems. I don't remember where daddy was when we heard the news that rocked the world. I remember sitting in the chair in front of our radio listening to something. I do not remember what. The program was interrupted for a statement by President Roosevelt. He announced that the Japanese had bombed some place called Pearl Harbor. Pearl Harbor belonged to the United States and President Roosevelt was mighty upset. Mama was in the kitchen and I told her. I remember she was drying a plate with a cloth and she stopped and just stood there for a minute with that blank stare she got from time to time when mulling over a problem. I did not know the location of Pearl Harbor, but I did know the President projected a lot of ill will toward the Japanese. I hunted up my geography book. In those days the study of geography was important. Mama and I found Pearl Harbor. We saw it in the book and on the map, but, honestly, neither of us had any idea of Hawaii's location.

*   *   *   *

Chapter 10

Christmas 1941 was the beginning of a very good year for me. World War II had just begun for Americans. The depression ended with a bang, not only for me but also for all Americans. We were operating in what we know now as a "war time economy." As hard as it was to believe, we were unable to keep up with the demand for hogs. Daddy had money in his pocket and in the bank. We never trusted a bank with our money during the '30s. Of course, we had no money in the '30s. I told you earlier about daddy's twenty-dollar bill. In those days that was money.

On Christmas morning Geraldine and I woke up Joe and looked in amazement at the full stockings hanging from the mantel over the fireplace. The previous Christmas, as great as it was, did not compare with what I saw. I could tell at a glance there were at least three oranges in my stocking. One was the most I ever found in a stocking in any past Christmas. And, oh my goodness, there were bananas also, and a bunch of all-day suckers, the yellow ones. On the hearth under each stocking sat a sack of chocolate drops, which we innocently referred to as "nigger toes." These chocolate drops were cream-filled, chocolate-covered, and cone-shaped, with a quarter-inch or half-inch cap of the cream poking through the chocolate at the point of the cone. It represented the toenail. Those were the good ones, not the cheap fakes we got back in the '30s. Each was about the size of a nickel at the bottom, tapering to a point about an inch or an inch and a quarter from the base. My excitement was so overwhelming I do not remember if I looked at Joe and Geraldine immediately to see if they had made out as well. I quickly peeled a huge banana and tossed the peel into the fire. I sat on the floor eating the banana and watching the peel turn black and shrivel up in the hot coals. One seldom had the good fortune to find a banana on Rawls Creek, and I had three.

Finally, with my mouth stuffed with rich, ripe banana, I glanced in Geraldine's direction to take inventory of her Christmas morning bounty. Her stocking hung unnoticed from the mantel as she purred and cooed over a new doll. It was as big as a small baby. Its eyes opened when the doll was moved to an upright position, and closed when the doll was prone. I found her absolutely enthralled, and for once exhibiting no desire to scream. Joe, I noticed, had crammed a handful of "nigger toes" into his mouth, so many he could not close it. Melted chocolate ran down his chin, and with the back of his hand he smeared it all over his face. His hand held a small red truck that he began to beat against the floor.

The doll and truck aroused my curiosity enough to cause me to search about for some sort of toy for me. It was standing in the corner of the stairs and the wall beside the fireplace. I did not believe what I saw. There it was, a Daisy Red Ryder repeater BB rifle. I had seen them advertised in my Red Ryder comic books but never had I seen the real thing. I often brought the subject up but always the answer was the same from mama. "No, no, he will shoot his eye out," she would tell daddy.

Leaping to my feet I lunged to the corner and grasped the wonderful Red Ryder BB gun with both hands. The barrel felt smooth and cool, as did the wooden stock. I felt happier than I had ever been. I did not know mama and daddy were in the room until I heard mama shout, "Don't point that thing at Joe. He will shoot his eye out, CS."

I never shot my eye out. Daddy and I spent many hours learning how to use the gun. He did a good job of teaching me safety. I still love guns, and until you boys came along they were everywhere in the house. Now, even you cannot get your hands on any of them.

During Christmas and into the second week of January 1942, snow successfully kept the ground covered. I did most of my practicing with the faithful Red Ryder BB gun in the barn. The sun showed its face the third Friday in January, and by Saturday afternoon much of the snow had melted. Sunday afternoon it warmed up considerably for winter in January. I put on my jodhpurs, my lace-up boots with the pocket for my Tree Brand knife, and my heaviest flannel shirt. Mama insisted I wear a denim jumper and cap with ear flaps. Decked out in this manner, I set out along the creek bank with my fully loaded Daisy Red Ryder repeater BB gun in search of game or Germans and Japs.

The water rushed by with a roar as I crept along the bank of Rawls Creek. Sheltered by the huge trees, mostly cedar, elm, hackberry, and occasionally sycamores, I parted the reeds, cane, and weeds to stalk the game or enemies that came to the creek to drink. I clutched my weapon tightly and held it at the ready. Occasionally I checked the pouch on my tightly laced boot to make sure the Tree Brand knife was there and ready for any up-close need. The underbrush was thick near the creek. Small branches and limbs slapped at my face and tugged at my clothing. I tried to brush them aside while clinging to my weapon. Carelessly I stumbled into a thicket of stick-tights. They were sticking to my clothes everywhere. I wondered how much the stick-tights would upset mama.

Suddenly there was a flash of blue just ahead. It settled on a small branch as I brought my weapon to the ready. Quickly aiming, I fired in one lightning-fast, liquid-like movement. The blue prey toppled off the branch and fell to the ground. I dashed madly ahead without regard to any other enemies such as Germans and Japs that might be lurking in the underbrush. There it was, my enemy. It flopped and flipped in the tall grass for a few seconds, then lay still and looked at me through its dark uninjured eye. My aim had been unerringly good. The eye asked me why. Fleeting surges of regret and shame shot through my body before settling in my stomach. As quickly as they came, the thrill of the kill and the vanquishing of my enemy overcame regret and shame. I fired a couple of rounds into the air to celebrate my arrival as a slayer of game and enemies.

I proudly showed my vanquished foe to mama. Her eyes glazed. She looked at me sadly, and without her saying a word, her eyes and face asked, "Why did you kill a bluebird?" I had no answer then or now. It's been many years, but still when I make a gross mistake I again wonder, "Why did I kill a bluebird?"

*   *   *   *

Spies Everywhere.

July heat burned off the chiggers, which we counted an advantage, one of the few advantages of the temperature soaring to nearly a hundred degrees. Certainly the corn and tobacco crops did not find advantageous the moisture being sucked out of the ground, withering their roots, by the blast-furnace heat. The rattlesnakes up on the Cub Nob, named for the last bear cub found in the area some years previously, were restless and traveling down the hill in search of cooling water. Daddy and I had killed two by the time July was half over.

"The sun just b-b-burned us another duster," Wilse said. Uncle Sam Enoch said, "I grabs, it's hot." Uncle Sam was right. I grabs, it was hot. It cooled off at night, not much but an improvement over the afternoon sun. Late afternoon and early evening I listened to the radio. We had the battery-powered Philco. We did not have electricity at this time, but I believe we had had the radio since late 1938 or early 1939. My favorite program other than "The Shadow" and "Captain Midnight," was Gabriel Heater with the news. "Ah, there's good news tonight." Or many times during part of the war it was "Ah, there's bad news tonight." That was the way he started his broadcast of the news each night. He kept me up to date on the war. I think Wilse listened to him also.

Heater was, in my opinion, better than Walter Winchell, who opened his broadcasts with "Good evening, Mr. and Mrs. America, and all the ships at sea." I always thought Heater was more serious in his news coverage. He reported several times that German U-boats, or submarines, had been spotted off the coasts of Maine and North Carolina. He reckoned they were dropping off spies and saboteurs to do dirty work in America.

The U.S. government had already picked up all the Japanese and Japanese-Americans they could find and put them in detention camps to keep them from helping the Japs against us. Wilse and I figured the Germans were trying to stir up the Germans living in the U.S. to help them in the war. Wilse had no use for the Germans, regardless of where they lived, and was of the opinion they needed to be in jail along with the Japs. Wilse figured they were putting the spies in the wrong locations. As he often told me, "We all know there is nothing worth a fart in N-N-North Carolina and damn few Germans." Maine was a vague area to both Wilse and me, but after looking in my geography book, Wilse felt it was damn well behind even N-N-North Carolina.

*   *   *   *

A spy in a tree

Mama, Joe, Geraldine, and I stood on the front porch looking over toward the hills above Wilson Marks' house. From our side of the valley the hills seemed to me to be cool, cooler than our side with the sun beating down on us with a vengeance. I wondered what it would be like to be on that hill. What was on the other side? I had never been there and always wondered what lay just over the next hill. I had been all the way to the top of Cub Nob. There was nothing on that hill but snakes, no bears anymore. They were all killed before I was born. Same way with the deer. They were all killed. Heck during the '30s nearly all the rabbits, squirrels, even ground hogs, were eaten to near disappearance. Skunks were hit hard also, but not for food. Block Brothers in Nashville would pay twenty-five cents for a good skunk pelt. Every barn on the creek had several boards for stretching and drying pelts hanging from a big nail on the sunny side. A 'possum would bring ten to twelve cents if anyone wanted to mess with a 'possum. Personally, I stayed away from both 'possums and skunks wherever and whenever possible. Things were different in 1942. Food was plentiful, but rabbits and squirrels still tasted good, and I still wondered what lay just over the next hill.

I decided to take a hike to the top of the hill on the other side of the valley. I explained to mama that I would climb to the top of a tree and wave my handkerchief at her to let her know I was there. She agreed to watch for me and wave her apron when she saw me. Then I would come home. I walked down the road to the house where my grandmother and Uncle Sam and Aunt Babe lived, crossed the creek, and climbed the hill up to Wilse's spring. I went into the spring house, lay on my belly, and took a drink of the cool spring water. I noticed two quarts of a clear liquid setting in the pool of spring water. I took it to be Wilse's gum medicine. One jar was only half full.

I walked up to Wilse's house and spoke to Mrs. Cowline and Lassie Lee before going on up the hill behind the house. In my memory, the hill across the valley from our house was a considerable hill and tolerable (a word we used in those days) steep.

I vividly remember the gnats and sweat bees that plagued me all the way up that hill. Although I was in thick woods, the shade was of little benefit. Cedar trees shed on me, thorn and locust trees scratched and poked me, stick-tights and buck bushes tore at my knees and ankles, making me wonder why I wasn't at home taking a nap under the dining table. Then I remembered I wanted to see what was on the other side of the hill, plus wave to mama. My desire to see what lay over the hill pushed me on more than my desire to wave to mama. The extreme heat encouraged me to turn back, but the new adventure caused me to persevere. My knees, skinned by the rocks I stumbled over, bled and ached. Numerous times rabbits, squirrels, and ground hogs startled me. Once a gray fox dashed out of a den practically under my feet. Scared the pee out of me, it did.

At long last I reached the top and located a clear space with a view of the other side of the hill. I looked out over a valley and more hills very much like the hill on which I was standing. I could see no houses, no towns, nothing except another hill and another and another. Disappointed, I climbed a big oak tree and faced my house across the valley on our hill.

As promised, I waved my handkerchief. There was no reply from mother, no acknowledgment that she could see me. I could see the house but did not see mama on the porch. I knew she would not forget to watch for me. Perhaps my handkerchief was too small. I took off my shirt and waved it back and forth several times. The answering wave of mama's apron came and I felt happy and relieved. Now I could go home out of the heat and take a nap under the dinner table. The floor was hard but cool. What I wanted then more than anything was cool.

*   *   *   *

Things I learned later

Tom and Wilse were resting comfortably in their rocking chairs, enjoying the full feeling from a recent meal Mrs. Cowline dutifully prepared and served. Both were smoking, Wilse his pipe and Tom a handmade coffin nail. Tom's eyes were closed.

"Look at that, Tom," Wilse said.

"Whut is it?" Tom asked without opening his eyes.

"A b-b-bunch of our idiot n-n-neighbors and their d-d-dogs".

Tom opened his eyes and saw three or four Mofields, two Kinslows, and a Bennett, all armed with shotguns and rifles.

"You don't suppose that bunch wants to go hunting, do you?" Tom asked. "It's too hot to find any animals out of their holes."

"None of them too d-d-damn smart, Tom."

"Hey Wilse, you and Tom get your guns and come on with us. There is a damn German spy up on the hill. We saw him up in a tree signaling to another one somewhere. We going to shoot his ass off. Come on, we don't have much time or he will get away."

"J.R. Mofield, what the hell is a German spy going to spy on from up a tree on that hill?" Tom asked.

"Going to spy on us, Tom. You ought to know. You fought the Germans last time. Now come on, we got to go."

"Me and pap going to sit this one out. Like you said, I fought the Germans last time. I never saw one up a tree though. Now go on, get him."

The little posse stumbled on behind their barking dogs, followed by three or four Mofield and Kinslow kids. Mrs. Cowline came out on the porch. She stood beside the kitchen door, polishing a plate with her drying cloth, and watched the posse disappear into the woods.

"What was that all about?" she asked.

Wilse sucked on his pipe and blew smoke out of both nostrils. "Just our local f-f-fools," he muttered.

"Said they got a German spy up a tree signaling to another one," Tom said.

"Why that's little James Winfree. Came by here about two hours ago saying he was going to climb a tree on top of the hill and wave to his mama. You should have stopped them, Wilson. They'll shoot James."

"Ain't going to s-s-shoot nobody 'cept maybe each other. That b-b-bunch couldn't catch a cold. Sure can't catch James. I'll bet he is home t-t-taking a nap under the table."

*   *   *   *

The Great Bus Wreck and Trial

After Aunt Belle and Uncle Bedford moved to the little rock house about half way between Rome and Hundley's Motel and Cafe, daddy and I had an opportunity to sit through two or three days of court in Carthage. Uncle Charlie was on jury duty and we were interested in the big bus wreck witnessed by Uncle Bedford. In those days one found very few people like Uncle Bedford. For that many people gave thanks. I don't mean anything bad by that, just that differences in people do exist, and we all should be thankful they do. Life could be boring otherwise.

Uncle Bedford never had much to say and took his time saying it, much to the frustration of the Nashville lawyers representing the Greyhound bus company in the lawsuit resulting from the wreck. I don't remember their full names, but one skinny little fellow was Jeffery. There was a tall lawyer with him. Solon Fitzpatrick was the lawyer for the plaintiff, Mr. Kittrell. He was a farmer who lived across Highway 70 from Uncle Bedford, not directly, but at about two o'clock, as we gave directions based on standing in the center of a clock dial and facing the twelve.

These were the facts as filed with the court. At approximately 9:25 a.m. on the day in question, the Greyhound bus, traveling at a high rate of speed, struck the rear of a wagon belonging to Kittrell. The wagon was loaded with freshly cut tobacco. The wagon and tobacco were destroyed. The accident grievously distressed the mules pulling the wagon by causing the wagon to strike them with great force, causing them to run with the remains of the wagon, the tobacco, and Kittrell almost to White's Service

Station. At a point almost in front of Kittrells barn, nothing remained of the wagon for Kittrell to sit on. After a few feet of grinding his rear end on the road he freed himself from the reins and abandoned the entire venture.

I cannot vouch for a report that Kittrell was seen dashing to the watering trough near his barn with his pants on fire. But he was observed sitting in the trough shortly thereafter. Kittrell carried the matches for his pipe in the pocket on the seat of his overalls. It is possible that the skidding on the pavement caused the matches to ignite, thereby setting fire to a strategic part of his overalls.

It was alleged by the bus company that a wagon driven by one Bedford Marks, headed in the opposite direction from Kittrell, was stopped, as was Kittrell's wagon, and the men were talking and blocking the highway unlawfully and illegally. Marks, having delivered his load to the barn, was returning for another load and met Kittrell on his way to the barn.

Uncle Charlie came out of the jury room and joined us waiting for the bus trial. Daddy asked why he was out of the jury room.

Uncle Charlie said, "That bunch of idiots don't like my brand of justice, so the judge fired me. I told him he was, by God, gonna pay me my juror's fee. He agreed. Said it would be little enough to get rid of me."

Daddy asked what he had done, but before he could tell us, the judge came out and banged his gavel for Kittrell vs. Greyhound.

Kittrell, puffing on his pipe, took his seat in the witness chair after swearing on the Bible he would tell the truth and nothing but. Solon Fitzpatrick, wearing a seersucker suit, walked up to Kittrell and began asking him questions.

Basically, his answers were: "Yes, the bus ran over me. Yes, it tore up my wagon. Yes, it tore up my tobacco. Yes, it hurt my mules and me. No, Bedford and I were not stopped, just passing, and I waved at him as he was going by."

Solon didn't have any more questions and said he just might rest after the other lawyer finished asking Kittrell questions.

The skinny Nashville lawyer, Jeffery, looked surprised, and walked right up into Kittrell's face and said, "You weren't stopped in the road?"

"Nope." Kittrell blew a cloud of Prince Albert smoke right into the lawyer's face. Jeffery choked and coughed while stepping back a few feet.

"I have a bus driver who will testify that you and the other wagon driver were stopped and jawing with each other."

Kittrell didn't say anything.

"Well, what do you think of that, Mr. Kittrell?" The skinny little lawyer was almost yelling. I noticed Slicker Huffines straighten up in his seat and write something on his pad. Slicker wrote for the newspaper.

"Think of what?"

"What I just said, Mr. Ktitrell. The bus driver will testify that you and Marks was both stopped. Blocking the road, both lanes."

"Will he, now?" Kittrell asked.

"Yes, he will. How does that make you feel?" The lawyer lowered his voice. "Well, how does that make you feel?"

"How does what make me feel?"

"Knowing he is going to say you aren't telling the truth. He's going to say you were stopped."

"Is he, now?" Kittrell just looked at Jeffery for a minute. "He the one what run over my ass?"

"Yes, you clod, that is the one." The lawyer was yelling.

Quicker than a flash Solon was on his feet, bristling and waving his hands and objecting for a lot of reasons. The judge beat his desk with the gavel and told Solon to sit down, and the Nashville lawyer to come up to his desk.

Uncle Charlie said, "That little fart shouldn't of called Kittrell a clod. Judge giving him a talking to."

"I don't think Solon is going to put Bedford on the stand," daddy said. "That is what all these people came here for. I wonder why not?"

"Hell, you know, CS. Solon too smart to use Bedford unless he just has to. No telling what Bedford would say. Probably take the rest of the day to get him to say it."

The judge made the Nashville lawyer apologize to Kittrell before he could ask any more questions. It went against Jeffery's grain to have to apologize to a clod like Kittrell, but he did.

Kittrell said, "You don't have to apologize to me. It ain't your fault you only got a blind witness like that ass hole."

Now the skinny lawyer was jumping up and down, telling the judge to chastise Kittrell for making that remark about the bus driver. The people in the courtroom were enjoying the excitement loudly, causing the judge to beat on his desk with the gavel. In a few minutes everything quieted down and the judge gave Kittrell a sour look.

"Mr. Kittrell, you apologize to the bus driver. You know he ain't blind. Maybe needs glasses, but he ain't blind."

Jeffery and the other lawyer that came with him were both on their feet and objecting loudly. The judge banged his gavel and the spectators roared with laughter.

The tall lawyer yelled, "I am not objecting to him calling the driver blind, your honor. It's the ass hole I'm objecting to."

"Hold it, hold it, Mr. Nashville lawyer!" said the judge. "We ain't having none of that kind of talk in my courtroom. Another outburst like that and I will have Sheriff Gann escort you to our fine jail."

It took a few minutes of gavel banging to get everything under control. The tall lawyer's face had turned purple and it was all the skinny fellow could do to get him seated. About that time Kittrell asked him a question.

"Why you objecting to the ass hole? He ain't said nothing?"

The judge declared a recess for fifteen minutes and the sheriff enforced it. We stood and stretched our legs, but no way were we going to leave our seats. The rest of this trial was going to be a show for sure and certain. Daddy waved at Slicker and even nodded at Dr. Reed. Dr. Reed ran the drug store on the square and had come over for a little fun. Reed Bros.

Drug Store was a Rexall drug store. I thought that Rexall was the company that made drugs. I thought that because every town had a Rexall store.

Slicker Huffines scribbled furiously in his notebook. Slicker had written an article about red worms some time before, and still referred to it often in his other articles. It was Slicker's opinion that man would ruin the earth in another fifty or sixty years and would become extinct like the dodo bird. After man was gone, the animals would go next, and after another hundred years, there would be nothing living on the land except red worms. He said that came straight from the Bible, King James version, where it says, "The meek shall inherit the earth." Nothing is meeker than an earthworm or red worm, said Slicker.

"Man doesn't know one end from the other and that is his downfall," wrote Slicker. "Not so with the red worm because it makes no difference to him. One end is as good as the other."

"All rise, all rise," the sheriff yelled as the judge re-entered the courtroom. Everyone settled down and Jeffery was back at Kittrell.

"In a few minutes I am going to call the driver of the bus to testify, and he is going to say your wagon was stopped in the road, blocking the lane. Do you want to change your testimony?"

"No. If you don't believe me, why don't you ask Bedford? He was right beside me when the bus hit me, and that is him sitting there in the folding chair."

"Why don't your lawyer call him to back up your story. He says he is going to rest his case without calling any other witnesses. Are you afraid of what that witness will say?"

"No. I don't need him to tell me I was not stopped. I was there. I know."

Solon Fitzpatrick was on his feet and shaking his finger at the skinny lawyer. Solon yelled, "I don't need you to tell me how to run my case. Looks to me like you have your hands full with a driver that needs glasses. Driver that can't see, driving a bus with people on it. That is probably a violation of some law. I better—"

Both Nashville lawyers were up and yelling at Solon. The judge started the gavel banging again.

"I never said he couldn't see," Jeffery shouted. "I never said he needed glasses. Someone else said that and didn't know what he was talking about. By God, I believe it was the judge. Hell's he butting in about this? None of his business." At that point the tall lawyer shoved skinny into his chair, nearly breaking it.

"I am sorry, your honor. Jeffery just got carried away and we apologize."

I don't think the judge could hear anything with all the laughing and yelling going on, not to mention the gavel banging. Finally the sheriff got things quieted down and the judge gave them all a scathing stare. Solon had some more things he wanted to say to Jeffery, but the judge told him to sit down and be quiet.

"Mr. Jeffery, Mr. Kittrell has told you several times his wagon was not stopped and I believe he will tell you that every time you ask him. My ruling is that you don't need to ask him again. Do you have any other questions?"

"No, your honor."

"Good. Cross examination is over. Do you have any other witnesses, Solon?"

"No, your honor. The plaintiff rests."

Jeffery got right to work and called the bus driver to the stand. After he was sworn in his testimony went something like this. He said he didn't wear glasses, didn't need glasses, could see perfectly well. Been driving a bus for eleven years and never had an accident before. Came over the rise and there were two wagons parked in the road, blocking both lanes. There was a high bank on the right side of the road and a ten-foot drop on the left. He couldn't stop and the choices weren't good. Go up the bank and turn the bus over, go on the left and turn the bus over, hit the Marks wagon head on into the mules, or hit the other wagon in the rear. That was what he did.

*   *   *   *

Uncle Bedford takes the stand

Jeffery and the tall lawyer got their heads together after Solon said he didn't have any questions on cross examination. They talked so long the judge asked them if they needed a five-minute break. They declined and asked the judge if they could approach the bench. They whispered to the judge a minute or so before returning to their end of the lawyers' table.

"Call Bedford Marks to the stand, sheriff," said the judge.

Uncle Charlie grinned and said, "Hot damn!" Daddy shook his head but said nothing. I knew he was pleased. It was always fun to see strangers tangle with Uncle Bedford. The spectators all smiled and made themselves as comfortable as possible.

"Have you fellers interviewed this witness?" the judge asked as Uncle Bedford made his way to the witness stand. "It might be a good idea to take a minute or two before you start." The judge was trying to help them.

Jeffery said, "No. We just want to ask him one question after he is sworn in and identified, as the law requires. Matters can't possibly get any worse."

"Now, Mr. Marks, I believe you know Mr. Kittrell. Is that correct?" Jeffery asked.

"Yes," said Uncle Bedford.

"And you helped him haul his tobacco to the barn, right?"

"I did."

"And you were present at the accident site at near 9:25 a.m. on that Wednesday morning?"

"Yes."

"Please tell us how you came to be there and what happened when you stopped to talk to Mr. Kittrell." This turned out to be one of Jeffery's more unfortunate questions, at least for him.

"I believe it was about 5:30 Tuesday evening when Kittrell came by the house. Might have been 6:00. No, we always eat at 6:00 and Belle was still cooking, so we hadn't eaten. So it must have been 5:30. Kittrell walked over with his old dog. It is not far from my house to where Kittrell lives. Just across the highway, in fact. Well not exactly across the highway. Sort of on a diagonal. You know diagonal, don't you? Not straight. Sort of slants off one way or another. In this case from my house it sort of slants off to the right. T'other way from Kittrell's place.

"Kittrell said he'd cut his tobacco and it was spiked, staked, and stuck in the ground. The black boys from over at Bellwood had helped him with the work. I've used them myself. Must be about a dozen of them. Some may be twins. Course they all look alike, them black boys do.

"Well, course I told Kittrell I would help him if it didn't rain. I don't like to—"

"Mr. Marks, please Mr. Marks. Were you there?" It was Jeffery interrupting Uncle Bedford, a bad move on his part. We all knew that.

"Whar?"

"The accident with the bus and the tobacco wagon, for God's sake."

Uncle Bedford sized Jeffery up before answering with a question of his own. "Do you mean was I helping Kittrell haul his tobacco?"

"Well, yes, of course that is what I mean." Jeffery was sort of agitated it seemed.

"I thought I told you about that."

"No, sir, you didn't tell me about that. Please answer the question."

"Do you mean the one about was I helping Kittrell haul his tobacco?" Uncle Bedford liked to make things clear.

"Yes, Mr. Marks, that is the question."

"I believe it was about 5:30 Tuesday evening when Kittrell came by the house. Might have been 6:00. No, we always eat at 6:00 and Belle was still cooking, so we hadn't eaten. So it must have been 5:30. Kittrell walked over with his old dog. It is not far from my house to where Kittrell lives. Just across the highway, in fact. Well not exactly across the highway. Sort of on a diagonal. You know diagonal, don't you? Not straight. Sort of slants off one way or another. In this case from my house it sort of slants off to the right. T'other way from Kittrell's place.

"Kittrell said he'd cut his tobacco and it was spiked, staked, and stuck in the ground. The black boys from over at Bellwood had helped him with the cutting and would be there tomorrow to load and unload. I can't remember the black boys' names. They are good workers. I've used them myself. Must be about a dozen of them. Some may be twins. Course they all look alike, them black boys do.

"Well, course I told Kittrell I would help him if it didn't rain. I don't like to work in the rain. Plus it ain't a very good idea to put up the tobacco when it is wet. Better to leave—"

"Mr. Marks, just answer the question. Were you there?" I thought Jeffery was going to have a stroke. The spectators were quiet but smiling broadly. Solon was twiddling his thumbs. The judge gazed at a dirty spot on the ceiling. Then Uncle Bedford answered again with a question.

"Whar".

"At the bus wreck, dummy, at the bus wreck!" Jeffery was yelling again.

"Don't badger your witness, Mr. Jeffery," said the judge. "Let him answer your question."

"I am trying, your honor. God knows, I am trying."

"Do you mean the one about was I helping Kittrell haul his tobacco?" Uncle Bedford asked.

Jeffery nodded.

"I thought I answered that one."

"No, you didn't, Mr. Marks. You haven't even gotten to the correct day. Please just tell us did you see the accident while helping Kittrell haul his tobacco?" Jeffery spoke in sort of a plaintive tone.

"I believe it was about 5:30 Tuesday evening when Kittrell came by the house. Might have been 6:00. No, we always eat at 6:00 and Belle was still cooking, so we hadn't eaten. So it must have been 5:30. Kittrell walked over with his old dog. It is not far from my house to where Kittrell lives. Just across the highway, in fact. Well not exactly across the highway. Sort of on a diagonal. You know diagonal, don't you? Not straight. Sort of slants off one way or another. In this case from my house it sort of slants off to the right. T'other way from Kittrell's place.

"Kittrell said he'd cut his tobacco and it was spiked, staked, and stuck in the ground. The black boys from over at Bellwood had helped him with the cutting and would be there tomorrow to load and unload. I can't remember the black boys' names. They are good workers. I've used them myself. Must be about a dozen of them. Some may be twins—"

"Not that again, Marks. Just answer the damn question. Were you there? Were you there?"

"You are badgering the witness again, Mr. Jeffery," the judge said, "I won't tolerate that in my courtroom. And you spectators quiet down. I am tired of banging this damn gavel. I'll have the sheriff clear the courtroom unless the laughing and yelling stops."

"Whar?"

"Thar, dammit, thar!"

"Mr. Jeffery, I told you to quit badgering the witness. He is your witness and I believe he will answer your question if you don't interrupt him so much. Now I don't want to have to warn you again. Don't badger the witness. Understand?"

"Yes, sir, but will he answer in our lifetime?"

I thought the judge was getting upset with Jeffery and everyone else. Daddy said the judge was just having fun with the Nashville lawyers. He knew Uncle Bedford and how hard it was to get a quick answer out of him. Solon knew also. That was why he didn't call him to be a witness.

"Do you mean the one about was I helping Kittrell haul his tobacco?" Uncle Bedford still wanted to be sure he was clear on the question "If you do, I've been trying to tell you, but you won't listen to my answer."

"God knows that is what I have been trying to do, listen for your answer. Were you there, did you see the wreck, and was Kittrell's wagon stopped?"

"I believe it was about 5:30 Tuesday evening when Kittrell came by the house. Might have been 6:00. No, we always eat at 6:00 and Belle was still cooking, so we hadn't eaten. So it must have been 5:30. Kittrell walked—"

"No, damn it, not again! We know you hadn't had supper and we don't give a damn if you had breakfast, or what you ate. Just tell us were you there, what did you see, and was the wagon stopped? And don't ask 'whar' because it was 'thar' where the bus hit the frigging wagon right in the middle of the frigging road. A simple yes or no will suffice. Now answer the damn question!"

Jeffery, his honor, and Uncle Charlie were in danger of having a stroke, the spectators were wild, and Uncle Bedford was calmly waiting for the next question, or for a chance to answer the last one. Uncle Charlie was laughing so hard he was beginning to choke. The word "frigging" had gotten me confused. The judge wasn't too happy about that either.

"Jeffery, you have frigged your last frig in my courtroom! Sheriff, go over there and restrain that lawyer. Handcuff him to his chair if necessary. Make sure he remains seated and his mouth shut."

The tall lawyer leaped to his feet and began yelling at the judge loud enough to be heard over the din in the courtroom. "Your honor, how much was the wagon and tobacco worth? I'll write you a check right now and forget this bizarre trial."

Don't you know that brought old Solon to his feet? "Six hundred dollars. Six hundred dollars if its worth a dime," he shouted

The judge said, "This court don't take checks but there's a bank across the street. You can cash your check there."

"I'll take it," Kittrell yelled.

"I am not giving anyone a check for six hundred dollars," the tall lawyer said. "Maybe two hundred, but no more."

"Not enough, not near enough," yelled Solon Fitzpatrick.

"I'll take it," yelled Kittrell.

The judge took the tall lawyer, Solon, and Kittrell back to his office. Jeffery was still sitting in his chair, yelling, waving his right hand, and stomping the floor with both feet. The sheriff had used handcuffs to fasten Jeffery's left wrist to a hook in the floor. The sheriff went with the judge and left the skinny little lawyer firmly secured in his chair.

Uncle Bedford, figuring he was excused, walked over to Jeffery and started talking to him. As we were leaving, I passed by him and heard him saying, "Right after breakfast I hitched up my mules to the wagon and went over to Kittrell's. I guess it was about 6:00 a.m. No, probably 6:30, 'cause we always eat breakfast at 6:00 o'clock, and I had already eaten. Belle fixed some fried ham, country cured for two years—"

Going out the door I heard the lawyer scream in a high-pitched wail which sounded, as Wilse would say, like a calf d-d-dying in a thunderstorm.

*   *   *   *

Chapter 11

When I was about 10 or 11 years of age, I would walk over to Mrs. Mary Underwood's house to get the books she always had for me. She not only taught me to read but also gave me books she knew I would find interesting before encouraging me to read books I needed to read, but might find uninteresting if I had not been taught to enjoy words. The books I got were such as *The Grapes of Wrath, Magnificent Obsession, Pilgrims Progress, A Tale of Two Cities, The Man In the Iron Mask, Two Years Before the Mast, A Christmas Carol,* and I don't remember how many others. Many of the books she sold to me for a dime or a quarter, or whatever, just to make me realize how important books were and are. Since I paid for them, they seemed more important than if she just gave them to me. As a result, I still have many of them and will pass them on to you.

Mr. Earl Underwood always tried to get me into his shop to show me how to make and repair things. I tried to spend some time with him but I knew their daughter, Betty, wanted to sit in the shade of the big oak trees and talk. I wanted to do that also. She told me she wanted to go to college and be a teacher in a big school in a big town somewhere. I told her I wanted to climb the hills and see what was on +the other side. We often dragged out the geography book and looked for places Gabriel Heater and Walter Wenchell talked about on the radio. Betty did not have a radio because her grandmother, Milissa Highers, would not let one in the house. "Devil's work, nothing but Satan's handiwork," she would say. Mr. Earl had a radio in his shop and let Betty listen to it. Betty and I knew very little about the devil and did not see what a radio had to do with him.

One day we were looking at a map of Africa and talking about Rommel, the Desert Fox, a big German general, when I decided to tell her about my dream. I had a continuing dream about Africa. I stopped when I noticed the expression on her face change. "Don't look at me like that. I know people don't have continuing dreams," I said. (Forty years later a friend of mine said, when I told him the same story, "That is a well-known fact that not too many people know about.")

Nevertheless, I had this continuing dream over a period of eight to ten months. I dreamt I was in a great valley somewhere in Africa, completely surrounded by straight-up walls that were seven hundred to a thousand feet high. The valley was filled with bush, jungle, pastures, rivers, springs, animals, and birds—everything that was needed for life—but there wasn't an exit. No one in the valley knew what was on the outside. No one had a need to go outside, but everyone wanted to be able to go outside. It was sort of like being in a plush prison, I suppose.

"Are the people black? In your dream, are you black?" Betty asked.

"All the people are black, and although I never have any indication one way or the other, I don't think I am. Maybe I am invisible and looking down on the valley. I never see myself. Anyhow, a large group of people is assigned to develop ways to escape, or to see what is over the cliffs. There must be some sort of supervisory control that determines who researches the escape project, who farms, who does other work. I am always with the research group, but not in charge. They could use D. Poston. We always come up with only one solution: build ladders to climb out. But the difficult part is the length, or height, of the ladder. If it is built on the ground, there is no way to raise it. Days, months, maybe years go by until we learn how to construct a ladder in the vertical position. How this is done is never revealed to me. Time after time the ladders get to within fifty or sixty feet of the top and then collapse, hurling workers on the ladders to their deaths. Nevertheless, we aren't discouraged and we start work again."

The valley was ideal. No war or sickness, beautiful weather, friendly, honest, hard-working people who got along with each other. But we wanted to get out, to see what was outside. Was it the Garden of Eden? Was God explaining Adam and Eve to me? Was our original sin really our desire to get out of Paradise? I don't know. I only know that after almost a year of this dream reoccurring at least once a week, I never had another.

Betty suggested I keep this to myself or I would be toted off to Central State Hospital like Sally Kinslow. Be sure not to let her grandmother hear about my dream. She would proclaim it to be the devil's work and ban me from her property, even Mr. Earl's workshop.

✳   ✳   ✳   ✳

The dreams stopped long ago, but I still remember every detail, and now I'm searching for the meaning behind the dream. You know I spent the better part of eight years in Africa, hunting that dream. From the time I was your age I wanted to know what lay on the other side of the hill. I searched the United States, Europe, the Middle East, Mexico, and Africa trying to find anything other than just another hill.

✳   ✳   ✳   ✳   ✳

The Great Sausage Machine

My Uncle Joe, daddy's brother, was always looking for what was on the other side of the hill, and he found a pot of gold on the other side of a hill somewhere. He and Aunt Virginia did not have any children, so they would borrow me for a few days. They lived in Madison and Uncle Joe ran a Western Auto Store. Sometimes he would drive up to our house and not bring Aunt Virginia with him. He would help get my clothes together and take me home with him for a week. I liked it better when he came by himself. I would get to ride in the front seat of the car and sometimes he would let me drive a bit, or make me think I was driving.

Also, on those occasions when he was by himself, on the way back to Madison, he liked to stop in Lebanon at a little place called "The Beer Barrel" and have two bottles of beer while I had a Seven-Up in a squatty brown bottle. We would talk and eat a hot pickled sausage, a "speedie." That is what Uncle Joe called them, but "The Beer Barrel" called them something else.

Uncle Joe liked to tell tales, some true and some made up, while he drank his beer. One of his favorites was how he made all his money when he built the Panama Canal. It was a very interesting tale, maybe true, maybe not, or a little bit of both. True or not, I enjoyed his stories.

He encouraged me to tell tales or little incidents that occurred at school or on the farm. He would then help me improve them. They have to be more interesting or people won't enjoy listening, or reading when you write a book. I told him about Turner Mofield's sausage-making machine and he helped me improve on the action and excitement. We may have worked through three beers and two Seven-Ups. Then a better sausage-making tale arrived. Here is what I remember of the story, slightly improved, perhaps.

It was about the time I bit into my first speedie. It was quite a shock to my tender taste buds. While I strangled, coughed, and guzzled nearly all my Seven-Up, Darnell P. Jellico eased into one of the extra chairs at our table. He took a pull on his beer and said, "I'll tell you about sausage and them speedies. I, Darnell P. Jellico, am old, but once I was young.

"We lived on a farm and made sausage. You won't find our method written down anywhere, but it was our method. When the weather in November got real cold, we'd have a hog-killing. About five or six of pap's farm neighbors would get together and kill hogs. I won't go into the scalding, scraping, gutting, and cutting up of the meat. It's the sausage you are interested in. We had no electricity back then, so we had to grind the sausage by hand. Guess who got that job? Us boys. It was hard work turning the sausage grinder all day by hand.

"Turner and me figured out a way to ease the labor a bit and speed up the work at the same time. We replaced the handle on the sausage grinder with a pulley off an old binder, jacked up Turner's old man's car, used a short, wide belt from the sawmill, and hooked it all up: rear wheel of the car and pulley on the grinder, with belt around both. We made it nice and snug so it wouldn't slip or jump off.

"We started the car, and when Turner put it in gear, that sausage mill began to turn at a ferocious speed. I put a piece of meat in the grinder and zap it was gone in a split second. Turner said we were going to need a hopper to feed that thing, so we built a hopper out of an old cream separator.

"We tried it out on a couple of pieces of meat and it worked fine. Pretty soon the men brought the meat all cut up for the sausage and we explained our idea. All the women folks came also to pack and bag the sausage. Everyone gathered round to see this sausage grinder get it on. Counting the kids, there was probably fifteen or twenty people crowded in front of the sausage grinder. Mr. Mart filled the hopper with two or three gallons of meat cut into little squares about two or three inches. Turner slid the car into gear and just let it idle slowly. Well, sir, that sausage came out fine and went right into the tub. Those people marveled and filled the hopper again.

"Old Hamp yelled for Turner to rev it up a bit and get the sausage made even quicker. Now they had about four gallons of cut-up meat in the hopper. Turner pushed the throttle wide open.

"It was a disaster of monumental proportions. That sausage came out in a stream about twenty miles per hour. It hit Mr. Mart's wife full in the face and curled all around her head and under her bonnet. She never did find her glasses. The bench where the grinder was attached sort of bounced around, and the stream of pork got Lena, Mr. Mart, Florence and Nevie. Poor Mrs. Lillie May was a little bitty woman, and when the sausage hit her, it knocked her down. Nearly all the kids got covered also. J.R.'s pack of coonhounds came alive and just about ate Mrs. Lillie May. Just about that time Newell drove up in his old A-Model Ford truck and he had five hounds with him and they joined the melee, thus provoking J.R.'s hounds into a real fight over the meat.

Well, they was some kind of screaming and yelling, growling and barking, a fair to middling amount of cussing. Babies began to scream and rub sausage in their eyes. Turner looked at me and the mess and said, 'Let's git.' We got.

"We spent the night in Kinslow's barn."

Uncle Joe, Bernard P. Jellico, and I agreed it was a better story than my version that was merely Turner Mofield rigging up a motorized sausage grinder.

Now I will tell you about the time Uncle Joe found a sack of fertilizer, a hundred pounds it was, and put it all on two or three pumpkin plants growing in aunt Virginia's garden. You wouldn't believe the size of those pumpkins. You can imagine the rest of this story and end it any way you like.

I liked Uncle Joe, and as I promised I never told daddy about "The Beer Barrel."

*   *   *   *

Chapter 12

Puberty was never mentioned in our house!

Suddenly I have lost control of my body. It is operating on its own. What is happening to me? I can feel my heart beating. I can feel the blood surging through my veins and arteries. Part of my body that does not usually move is moving on its own. I think my eyes have crossed. I have great feelings of ease and unease at the same time. My skin is hot and flushed. The pores are open and wet. I am sweating. Do I have a fever? I need some fresh air but I cannot move. My feet send roots deep into the floor and I feel I will never move again, at least in the direction of the door. I try to shake my head and it does not move. My eyes don't blink.

I have to think. I am in Mrs. Mary Underwood's parlor, where I have been many times before. The room remains as it was last week when I was here. Betty Underwood is with me, as she was then.

We are at the bookcases, looking for the books Mrs. Mary thinks I might enjoy reading. Betty is on the ladder that slides in front of the bookcases to make it easier to retrieve books from the topmost shelves. Her feet are about even with my head. She is searching for *Riders of The Purple Sage* and *Wildfire*, by Zane Grey, and *Gun Feud*, by E. B. Mann. I am looking up to see if she needs me to push the ladder in one direction or another. Am I having a heart attack? Numbness invades my whirling and churning brain. I look at Betty's legs, starting at the ankles that are almost at eye level, and move upward. They are beautiful legs, long and curvy. I am in awe of those legs. I have never seen anything so beautiful as those legs. My eyes move further up and I see her round, firm butt enclosed in silky panties. I nearly choke.

Zane Grey and E. B. Mann have disappeared from my mind in a flash, immediately replaced by this vision of unendurable beauty never before seen by me. I am twelve years old and Betty is probably eleven. We have been friends and played together all our lives. Only last week I saw Betty's legs and butt when she climbed the ladder to get *Arizona Ames* and *The Call of the Canyon* for me. There was nothing unusual about her legs and butt last week. They were perfectly normal legs and butt for an eleven-year-old girl. What has happened?

I hear a scuffling noise behind me and realize Betty's mother is in the room. My face ignites. It has never done that before. Betty's mother is often in the room with us. There is a mirror on the wall near me. I see my reflection and my face is scarlet. Why?

Mrs. Mary is a tall, handsome woman and she gave her good looks to Betty. Funny, I never noticed that before. The way she looks at me concerns me and I do not know why. She often looks at me. She smiles, almost giggles, and covers her mouth with her hand. She turns her eyes upward to speak to Betty.

"Have you found the books for James?"

"I see the last one, but I need a push over toward the window to be able to reach it," Betty says.

"Give her a push, James."

I fix my eyes firmly on the buckles of Betty's shoes and push the rolling ladder about one step toward the window. Betty removes the third book from the shelf, clutches it along with the other two to her chest, and turns around on the ladder. She glances at me, then leaps off the third step to the floor. Her skirt billows out and up, exposing those beautiful legs once again. With some difficulty, I stare at the ceiling. The leap from the ladder obviously startles Mrs. Mary, because she spins on her heel and dashes out the door. I hear her making noises outside. I cannot tell if she is laughing or strangling.

Betty presses the books on me and I want to kiss her, hug her, or run. I wish I were home, but I cannot stand the thought of leaving. My face is on fire again. Betty is staring at me. Her big blue eyes sparkle, then become serious, as if with concern. She places a beautiful white hand on my forehead and the fire in my cheeks rushes there.

"You feel hot, James. Do you have a fever? I do hope not. Our school play is next Friday and I cannot stand it if you are sick and that awful Mofield boy takes your place."

She is not alone. I cannot stand that either. The very thought of someone else in the play with her makes me sick. My situation is hopeless. If I can face Mrs. Mary I will ask her for an aspirin. Suddenly I am aware of Betty's hands on my cheeks, gently rubbing them as if to soothe or cool their fire. Though demoralized, unnerved, weakened, broken, and possibly unstrung, I see escape ahead. Run! I must run, and I do. My salvation is a mad dash for the fence, over it into the pasture, and then home and the safety of my room to think. I do not look back so I do not see the blank and confused expression on Betty's beautiful face. Nor do I see Mrs. Mary in a state of near collapse from laughter. Disturbed by the activity, Mr. Earl comes out of his workshop looking first at my fast retreat, then at his wife. Betty, unnoticed and as still as stone, hopes I will not lose the books.

*   *   *   *

That Awful Play

The entire community poured into the one-room schoolhouse on Rawls Creek. It was Friday night, late in October 1944. The room, brightly lighted by two gaslights with four mantles each, filled quickly. Trace chains suspended the big lanterns from the ceiling. Early that afternoon I had climbed the stepladder and filled the lights with fuel, and pumped up the pressure. John M. lit them just before people began arriving. Already people occupied most of the seats. My father, mother, Geraldine, my brother, Joe, and my new sister, Jean, occupied the front row on the right center of the room. No one expected this play to be an outstanding production, but it would take everyone's mind off the war in Europe and the Pacific for two hours.

Mr. Earl earlier that week had strung a large wire across the room. Mrs. Mary, with Mr. Earl's help, made a curtain of four bed sheets that now covered part of the room, including the stage. Behind the curtain all was nervousness. The actors were going over their lines. The stage crew was setting up tables and chairs while following directions given by Mrs. Mary in hushed tones. I was the star, so I got to sit in a chair and watch while avoiding Mrs. Mary's eyes. I looked at Betty as much as possible. From time to time, Mrs. Mary went to the door to greet people coming in. When she went on the other side of the curtain, Betty plopped onto my lap and kissed me on the lips. All the other kids said, "Whooo."

That was the end of a tumultuous week for both Betty and me. One week before I had no desire to kiss Betty and she had no desire to kiss me. Now we could not leave each other alone, regardless of how much the other kids giggled and pointed at us. I did not understand what had changed. I tried to talk to daddy about this, but he only patted me on the head and said, "You are growing up, son," That was little help. I did not try to discuss this situation with my mother. Women didn't understand such things. At school that week (I did not want to be there but daddy would accept none of my excuses) every time I looked at Mrs. Mary or she looked at me, I turned bright red. When she called on me to recite, I choked. No sounds came out of my mouth when I tried to talk. Two or three times she called me aside and tried to tell me everything was OK, that she understood, but I panicked and could not respond.

I sat there on the stage wondering if I would forget my lines when Betty said her lines to me. Probably. I can't remember them now. Mrs. Mary parted the curtains and went to see about extra seats for the overflow crowd. Betty dashed for my lap. She threw her arms around my neck and kissed me on the lips again. I patted her thigh. Clifton "Tit" Mofield pulled the rope attached to the curtain and opened the stage to full view. The entire audience burst into laughter and applause. Hearing the noise, Mrs. Mary spun on her heel and dashed toward the stage yelling for someone to close the curtains. Betty jumped out of my lap and bowed to the crowd, then jumped up and down while smiling and clapping her hands. I broke for the back door and headed for the road east toward Grant.

The wind whistled past my ears, and behind me I heard Mrs. Mary calling. Then I heard daddy join in the yelling. I paid them no heed and kept going full tilt. Inside the schoolhouse, pandemonium reigned. No one cared if they ever heard or saw the play. They had already had an enjoyable evening. About a quarter of a mile from the school, I heard footsteps behind me. I looked back and saw John M. gaining on me. John M. was about old enough for the military draft. I stopped and he slung me over his shoulder and took me back to school at a trot. Betty was glad to see me. Personally, I wanted to die.

The curtain was still open when John M. deposited me on the stage. Everyone applauded. Betty grabbed me again and asked, "Are you embarrassed for people to know I am crazy about you?" I did not reply.

The next two years at Rawls Creek School were glorious for me, and I hope for Betty. After that, we moved. I attended Lebanon High School while Betty finished Rawls Creek and attended Carthage High School, I think. I left home for Middle Tennessee State College, and after that, the Army for the Korean Conflict. Betty and I lost touch. I only saw her once after Rawls Creek School. I hunted her up and asked her to go to a MTSC football game with me. She accepted. I remember it as if it were today. She met me at the door of her house, tall and beautiful with the same long legs and big blue eyes. I choked.

As we looked for our seats in the student section, I noticed we attracted considerable attention. It was mostly Betty attracting the attention. I enjoyed the moment. I do not remember ever seeing her again after that day. I wonder why.

*   *   *   *

That gets me to thinking. I sort of liked Chat Agee also. She looked at me as if I were a lump of something gross. I don't know why.

Don't worry if people tell you they remember those days a bit differently than me. I may remember them as I wish they had been, but then maybe not. Time changes things in our minds, but I did like both Betty and Chat and still think of them now and again.

*   *   *   *

A Snake with Ears

The growing Winfree clan sometimes was short on toys, entertainment, almost everything growing boys and girls needed. We did have our imaginations and they were fertile. We created our own entertainment and toys. I had a horse that doubled as a broom, a rifle that looked very much like a broken stick, and a pistol carved out of a pine plank. Most of the kids I knew had similar toys, some more intricately carved than ours.

Four or five fruit trees grew in the corner of our yard, peach and apple. We called this the orchard. Using big cardboard boxes, we built a store and a bank. Our stock was rocks of different sizes, representing all sorts of canned goods and staples. One large rock was gold and was kept in the bank with smaller pieces of gold. Geraldine and Joe ran the store and I varied between robber, customer, and policeman. Whatever the game, Geraldine participated and played the role assigned to her by me. Joe was a different matter. First, he was young, and second, he was stubborn, always wanting to do things his way. Sometimes this was good and other times it was a disaster.

I well remember one day I was to be a bank robber and Joe the teller. I alit from my horse and dashed into the bank, guns drawn, yelling, "Give me your gold." Joe had his back to me but, without looking, he gave me the gold. Boy, did he! The rock, about the size of a small grapefruit, was on the table in the cardboard bank. The three-year-old for once did as instructed. He picked up the gold I wanted and tossed it over his shoulder rather vigorously. The gold struck me in the very middle of my forehead. I dropped my gun, fell on my butt, and passed out, wrecking the bank in the process. I remember Geraldine saying, "You've killed him." He had not, but I did not notice any remorse from him. After a bit, I got up and beat his butt.

We declared a truce, me with a gigantic lump in the middle of my forehead, Joe with little desire to sit anywhere, Geraldine unsure who to be mad at. We worked together to rebuild the bank. I learned from the bank robber's point of view the value of being able to see the bankers from the front. Rebuilding takes a long time because one has to unbuild before one can rebuild, and that slowed us down.

Joe yelled at me, "Jim, here's a snake with ears".

I found Joe behind a cardboard box he was moving. He was squatting, looking the big coiled snake eyeball-to-eyeball at close range. The snake, with its head thrust upward, and Joe were almost level with each other. The snake, a rattlesnake I am quite sure, did have ears and a large head. I grabbed Joe by the collar and jerked hard, throwing him behind me at least six feet. Geraldine had both hands filled with gold when she saw the snake. Reflex action caused her to chunk the gold as hard as she could at the snake. Both pieces found their mark and did the snake some damage. I think she made him belch, or at least open his mouth. When he did a rabbit hopped out. The snake had about half-swallowed the rabbit from the rear end, leaving his head, ears, and front legs hanging out of his mouth. Hence the snake with ears. I pummeled the snake with various canned goods and with my horse. (**I know snakes swallow their prey head-first, but this one was different for some reason. Maybe he was an ignorant snake. After all, he was trying to eat in a cardboard bank crowded with rowdy kids.**)

The rabbit half-hopped, half-crawled away as fast as possible into the high grass, but I think he was poisoned and unlikely to go far. The snake, no longer interested in the rabbit, began looking for a safer place. He also disappeared into the high grass, but he was not very swift. The gold and my horse injured him, and I am sure he perished.

Joe squealed like a fresh-cut pig as he sat on his recently tanned butt in pain and upset at being so rudely removed from the snake with ears.

It seemed Joe's lot in life was to be in close contact with snakes. I am surprised he didn't grow up to be a snake-handling preacher. Joe never actually handled snakes. He merely attracted them. Take a walk with Joe and snakes turned up. One day we walked down the hill to our other house, where mammy, Uncle Sam, and Aunt Babe lived. Uncle Sam was cutting grass in the yard with a Lively Lad sling blade. His back was to us when we heard him talking, to someone on the porch we thought. Getting closer, we saw no one on the porch or anywhere nearby. Then we heard what he was saying.

"I grabs, I'll cut your head off, I will. I grabs, I'll teach you to strike at me," Uncle Sam said. He took a ferocious whack at something in the grass. His back swing of the Lively Lad sling blade deposited something fairly close to Joe. I looked and saw about eight inches of a rattlesnake with head attached. I jerked Joe away so he would not try to pick it up. Snake heads will bite you for four hours after being removed.

Uncle Sam picked up the snake by the tail and counted its rattles. That snake measured a bit over five feet. "I grabs, he's a biggun," Uncle Sam said. "You want his rattle, James? You can scare girls with it." He cut it off, rattled it at Joe, then gave it to me. It had fourteen rattles and a button. I didn't really want it but I took it as a testament to manhood. Joe wanted it but I did not give it to him because he would probably eat it, as he did everything. He was not quite four years old.

*   *   *   *

More Snakes

On the backside of our farm was a field that usually lay fallow for three years. Then we would cultivate it for two years. The last year we lived on the creek, daddy plowed the field and planted it for hay. I think he planted it with a new strain of clover, but maybe not. Geraldine, Joe, and I carried him some water in the middle of a very hot afternoon. It was not a long walk. A round trip covered about half of a mile along a wagon road we built, or rather left uncultivated because we needed to get wagons to the field to haul the hay out and to get mowers in to cut the hay. Walking back, Joe ran several yards ahead of us because he would never listen to anything we told him about danger or Germans and Japs or snakes. He said, "I am five years old. I am not a baby." Well, he was not five yet, and he was still a baby.

Suddenly he stopped and stood peering into the tall weeds and grass on one side of the road. I caught up to him and I heard the familiar rattle emanating from the tall grass. "Not again," I said as I grabbed the little squirt by the shirt collar and threw him across the road onto the freshly plowed ground. I motioned for Geraldine to stay back, but that was not necessary. She was smart. Even the dumbest farm kid will learn something. If it is hot and dry on Rawls Creek, there will be snakes looking for water, and many of them will be rattlesnakes. I had counted twelve years of my life and was not dumb, so I carried a weapon. That day it was a grubbing hoe, and like Uncle Sam, I said, "I grabs, I'll cut your head off." I did. Then I told Joe to shut up his squalling and drag the snake for me.

We passed a pile of brush made from cleaning out what would have been a fence row if we had had a fence. I threw the snake onto the brush knowing daddy would burn it in a few days. One cannot leave a dead snake lying around, especially one as big as that particular snake.

Mama had a fairly early supper that day and a good supper it was, as I remember. Afterwards, we lazed around in the back yard enjoying the coolness of the early evening. The sun that burned us all day was setting and its heat dissipating into the cooling haze of pre-twilight. Joe by now had decided he had killed the snake and wanted to show it to daddy. While we looked at the snake lying atop the pile of brush, daddy decided we might as well burn it then. There was plenty of time before we went to bed for it to burn itself out. After about thirty minutes the fire began to die down and the snake dropped onto the hot coals. Ten seconds later the dogs, Jug and Pete, were up on their feet, looking as if they might leap into the fire. Even then my nose was a little slow on the uptake, thus I could not imagine the cause of the dogs' agitation. The snake was cooking and evidently it had a fantastic aroma. I didn't know because of my nose problem.

The problem with my nose started a year earlier at our other house, where we were living with mammy and Aunt Arther and Uncle Andy. It may have been Uncle Sam and Aunt Babe. I don't remember. At one time or another everybody lived there. Anyhow, I was chasing Geraldine on the L-shaped porch. She turned the corner and ran past mammy, who was just about to lift the section of the porch floor that was the door to the cellar. I arrived just after she opened the cellar door and went down the cellar steps nose first. It was a painful trip.

I climbed out of the cellar holding my crushed nose with my left hand while rubbing the rest of my battered body with my right hand. Mama heard mammy yelling, me crying, and the dogs barking, and came to my aid. She filled a wash pan with water from the cistern and washed the blood away from my mangled nose. Fresh blood flowed freely from my nose to replace what she washed off. She stopped the bleeding by plugging my nostrils with cotton. Now she looked at my nose and said, "Oh shit." It had moved over to the left side of my face. None too gently, I thought, she moved my nose back to its proper position, more or less. Mammy brought a roll of adhesive tape and the scissors. Together they put my nose where it is today. After about an hour, mama pulled the cotton from my nose to see if it worked. Let me put it this way. I could once again breathe through at least one nostril, and it is working today. But I don't smell odors very well.

Daddy could smell that snake cooking and understood Jug and Pete's agitation. He fetched a shovel from the corncrib and gave them each a shovel load of rattlesnake. It required five shovel loads to get the snake served to the dogs. Joe wanted a bite but I didn't. I now know rattlesnake is a delicacy and we missed some gourmet eating.

*   *   *   *

It is amazing how time affects one's memory. Not long ago Joe told a group of his friends he felt lucky to be alive after following me around when he was small. He said, "Jim attracted snakes like a magnet attracts steel. I really thought he would grow up to be a snake-handling preacher."

I should have left him standing on his head in the mud the time he fell off a mule we were watering. He was really too young to be riding a mule but he begged, so I let him. He was about eighteen months old. He sank in the mud about five inches and stood on his head, kicking his feet until he finally fell over into more mud. I cleaned him up as much as I could and told him that if he ever told daddy about falling off the mule, I would see that he never rode a mule again. Did he tell daddy? You bet he did. He told everyone at the dinner table, the blabber-mouth. Well, in truth, he did wait forty years before he told. He has not been riding a mule since he blabbed everything. I kept that promise.

*   *   *   *

Chapter 13

Before I was fourteen years old I witnessed one murder and committed three, if you count the bluebird but not rattlesnakes and pigs and such. I am now confessing and I hope you will forgive me. But if you don't, well, I don't care.

*　　　*　　　*　　　*

Murder in My Heart

Walking down the Rawls Creek Road, after passing Lee Mofield's place on the right and Jess Poston's place on the left, there was a long straight stretch of road ending in an S-curve near the creek. It had once been in the creek. At the end of the curve (incidentally, that is where daddy and Turner Mofield banged their cars together one time) a garage was located just barely off the road. On the hill above it was a large two-story house. I don't remember who lived there, but I never liked them.

I do remember walking at a good clip as I passed that garage the first morning on my way to catch the Trailways bus.

* * * *

Christopher may remember when he was four years old and we were playing hide-and-go-seek, how I yelled at him when he opened the closet door where I was hiding. He said, "Granddaddy, you scared the pee out of me."

I need to explain why I was walking to catch the Trailways bus. Daddy was a member of the county court fighting in support of the school board for school busses to transport pupils to and from school. Now that the war no longer prevented the production of school busses, he felt it ridiculous for Smith County children not to have transportation. He battled Hen Lancaster, a court member from Lancaster, and Webb Allen, a member from the Difficult and Defeated Creek area, I think.

Both men had blocks of support in the court, and combined, they were larger than daddy's block. He once said Hen Lancaster would squeeze a nickel until the buffalo shit. Daddy allowed he had no desire to drive me eight miles to Carthage High School.

Wilson County had school busses. Daddy found a small farm for sale near Tucker's Cross Roads in Wilson County, bought it, and we moved. In Wilson County the schools started in August, but we could not have possession of the farm until January. It was determined that I would ride the Trailways bus. I only had to walk one mile to the bus. What a lucky break!

* * * *

As I passed the garage, there arose a great screeching, flapping of wings, and flutter of feathers. All of this occurred just over my head. Like Christopher, it scared the pee out of me. I had to go home and change my pants, causing me to very nearly miss the bus.

It was a flock of guinea fowl. Guinea fowl are, so far as I am able to determine, totally useless and disgustingly noisy birds, especially the hens. Their screeching is intolerable. People that own them must be deaf or crazy, or both. To this day I detest guinea fowl.

It turned out the guinea screeching and attempting to fly was an every-day event. It didn't matter that I knew it occurred daily and always at the garage. I could not prepare myself for it. After a few weeks, the damn things grew more and more cheeky. They waited for me in the road and almost dared me to pass. Daddy suggested I take a stick with me and punch them out of the way. I tried the stick punching and only irritated them more.

Next, they began to lie in wait for me in the afternoon, especially two big bitches with a real desire to attack me. Whoever the people were that lived in the big house would, quite often, sit on the porch and laugh at me, the old farts. One Saturday I decided to take matters into my own hands. Using daddy's sharp double-bladed ax, I cut a small limb off of a hickory tree. I chose one with a big joint on the end connected to the trunk of the tree. With the hawk-billed knife Uncle Charlie gave me, I whittled that limb into a walking stick with a knob on the end about the size of a green apple. It was a replica of the one Wilse used.

There was a bridge over Plunkett's Creek, just before it ran into Rawls Creek and both went under the bridge on highway 70N. I made me a hiding place there to leave my walking stick. I didn't need it at school, at least I didn't think I did. I retrieved it every afternoon and prepared to do battle with the guinea hens. One afternoon I noticed the people who usually sat on the porch and laughed at me were not there. The garage doors were open and I figured that since the car was gone, so were they. As I neared the garage, two guinea hens strutted into the middle of the road, screeching and flapping, daring me to approach. Today, I thought, you have met your destiny.

Grasping my walking stick by the bottom end, I approached the hens. These were big birds, maybe five pounds or more, almost as big as a small turkey. One strutted out in front of me, screeched loudly, ruffled her wings, and flapped them as if to say, "You will not pass today." She was wrong. I held my walking stick much as your daddy holds his golf club just before making his tee shot. I swung it hard at the hen's evil, lemon-shaped head. Unlike your daddy with his golf club, I made a sweet, smooth, solid connection. The guinea hen's head received the full force of my swing. The disgusting fowl sailed five or six feet through the air until settling and flopping just inside the garage. It was a hole in one, as they say in golf.

I turned to face the other hen that was strangely silent, as were the spectator guineas. Screech at this, you bitch, was my thought as I took a mighty swing at her. The knot on the end of my stick cracked her head like mama cracked an egg against the old black cast iron skillet. No hole in one this time. This one went into a water hazard, a dried up ditch beside the road. My cup overflowed with joy for a long moment, and then came the realization of what I had done. I had killed someone's guinea fowl. As soon as they found the hens they would know who did it. From listening to "Mr. District Attorney" on the radio, I knew I must dispose of the evidence. Fortunately, Harrington, the DA's investigator, was not there to investigate me.

By the time the hens stopped flopping, I had a plan. The other birds, sensing a possible attack, had launched themselves into a sort of running flight, partly in the air and partly on the ground, amid a flurry of white-spotted, black-gray feathers. After reaching what they considered a safe distance, they settled in a huddle and remained strangely quiet. Slinging my book satchel over my shoulder and putting the stick under my arm, I picked up the hens by their feet and headed home. The cracked and damaged heads dragged and bounced along the road. I hoped I would not meet anyone on my trip home. I did not.

Mama is dead and gone now, and I can tell her part in this sordid deed without embarrassment or shame. Mama became a willing accomplice to my evil deed. As I lumbered along the old road up to our house, I met mama on her way down to mammy's place. What a surprise I was to her, my satchel slung over my back, a walking stick under my arm, a dead guinea hen in each hand. Additionally, I was hot and sweating and my arms ached from the weight of the hens. Just as George Washington could not tell a lie when caught with an ax in his hand and standing next to a freshly cut cherry tree, I couldn't either. Anyway, I had complained enough about the guinea fowl to preclude anything but the truth.

"James Lofton, what have you got in your hands?" You might consider that a rhetorical question, since my mother saw clearly the guinea hen in each hand. I had planned to throw them in the sinkhole to the left of the road about another fifty yards from where we stood

"I killed two of those damned guineas, mama. I am tired of them bothering me and those old farts laughing at me."

"That is no way to talk, James Lofton. Your daddy won't like that. What were you planning to do with the guineas?"

"Throw them in the sinkhole."

She took the hens from me and said, "Let's go home and think about this."

We did, but I did not do much thinking. After all, I got up at 5:00 a.m. to start my day and it then was after 6:00 p.m. I need rest.

Mama fired up the stove and filled a big galvanized bucket with water from the cistern. She put it on the stove to boil. Then she hunted up her ***Fannie Farmer Cookbook.*** It was the fourth revised edition, first published in 1923. Hers was a 1924 reprint. I stood there in amazement, shifting from one foot to the other. Sure enough, somewhere about page four hundred, appeared an entry entitled, "Guinea Fowl." The instructions were, "Roast like a chicken." Mama closed the book. She knew how to cook chicken. The water began to boil rapidly. Mama plunged one guinea hen into the boiling water and left it for a few minutes. Soon she removed it, and when the water returned to a rapid boil, she plunged the other fowl into the water. Now she tested the first one and easily removed a few feathers. She removed the second hen from the boiling water and took both out onto the back porch and hooked their feet in a wire hanging from a rafter. She proceeded to pluck the fowls until they were clean. On an oak cutting board daddy made for her, she gutted and cleaned the hens, then washed them thoroughly. She cut each into eight to ten pieces.

During this entire procedure, mama quizzed me about school, the bus ride, and what I ate for breakfast at Hundley's Motel and Cafe. I was dumfounded at the motel question. I expected a good raking over the coals.

She moved the pieces of the hen into the kitchen and seasoned them with salt and pepper. Next she placed then in a brown paper bag with a cup of flour and gave them a vigorous shake, then set the bag aside. "Stoke the stove, James." I did and she brought out the old black cast iron skillet, set it on the stove, and dumped a cup of lard into it. While the lard was melting, she chopped two onions. The onions went into the skillet, and when they were frying in very hot lard, she shook off the excess flour from the guinea fowl pieces and added them to the onions. As the pieces fried, mama sliced three carrots and put them in the skillet. She sprinkled rosemary, sage, and thyme into the skillet and added a couple of laurel leaves, along with two cups of chicken juice she always had in the warmer or the icebox.

"We will let this simmer for half an hour, then bake it until CS gets home. He went to Charlie's for something and took Geraldine and Joe with him. Florence wanted to see them. CS said he would be back about dark. If he asks about what we are eating I will answer him. You keep your mouth shut. Like they say on "Mr. District Attorney," we will dispose of the evidence before anyone knows murder has been committed. Those old farts should not have laughed at you."

I grinned from ear to ear and that was the best dinner I ever ate. Never again did the guinea fowl attack me. Neither did they screech at me. A few days later I observed one of the old farts counting the guineas. I smiled.

*   *   *   *

The Executions

I considered a disadvantage the mile walk to and from the bus each day. But the stop at Hundley's Motel and Café was a definite advantage. The bus traveled all night before it reached Hundley's. The people, hungry and in need of bathroom facilities, piled off the bus and into the café, quickly forming a line for the two small rest rooms. I usually picked a table near the window and got my coffee and doughnuts before the other passengers finished with the rest rooms.

One morning, as I sipped my coffee, I stared at the Rendezvous Club across the highway. Mama worried about me being so close to a beer joint with the reputation of the Rendezvous Club. She felt sure it would rub off on me. It may have. I remembered Uncle Charlie telling me there would be more killings at the Rendezvous Club when the war ended than there were in Germany. He said all the women with husbands in the war went there, drank beer, and then piled up in a bed in Hundley's Motel with some cripple or draft dodger, or an old fart like Herschel Mofield. Uncle Charlie was wrong. When the men came home from the war they were so glad to be home they didn't seem to care who had piled up with whom.

My reverie was disturbed by Mr. Hundley yelling, "Where did they go? They didn't have to leave that quick. I've got their damn food right now."

A meek voice answered Hundley's yell, "We didn't leave. We've just moved by the window."

I noticed there was a lot of confusion. The waitress was missing and Hundley was trying to serve the food. The tables were close together and Hundley's butt was too big to get between them. His shoulders were narrow enough, but being built upside down wouldn't let him between the tables. Across the room someone yelled about no gravy with his order of gravy and biscuits. Mrs. Hundley came prancing out of the kitchen. She was wearing an apron, spike heels, and a lot of flour on her hands, in her hair, smeared over the apron, and a bit on the toes of her shoes.

"Don't get your drawers in a wad, the gravy is coming now. I can't do everything," Mrs. Hundley yelled at the man wanting gravy with his gravy and biscuits.

I had not seen Mrs. Hundley in the kitchen before. Usually she was sitting on a stool, puffing on a Cool cigarette, and polishing her nails. The bus driver eased into the chair across from me with a cup of coffee and half a dozen chocolate doughnuts. "What's going on here this morning?" he asked. "I had to get my own coffee and doughnuts. I never saw that Hundley bitch do anything before except smoke and polish her nails."

"I don't know, but it sure is a mess. Listen to that guy over there. He wanted jelly doughnuts and got ham and biscuits. Said he was Jewish and couldn't eat that ham. Hundley's wife said she didn't give a damn about his religion. If he didn't want the ham, give to the black guy over by the coffee maker. He'll eat anything, she says."

Actually, she was right because I heard him yell, "Food, any food, just bring it to me. Leftovers, or whatever. I am starving."

About that time Hundley beat a serving spoon against the cash register and yelled for everybody to shut up. "We've got a problem this morning," he said. "My waitress is not here today because Kentucky executed her daddy at sunrise today. My cook ain't here either because they executed his brother, too. If you will just bear with us, we'll get you all taken care of as best we can."

Everyone quieted down and all got some food eventually. I knew I would be late for school because the bus driver went back for another half-dozen doughnuts. "Executed them at sunrise," he said. "Ain't that a kick in the ass? What you suppose they did?"

I sipped my coffee and let the question sort of die.

*   *   *   *